THE EARLY DAYS OF AUTOMOBILES

Around the track at 102 miles per hour came George Robert-son at the wheel of his demon Locomobile. The year was 1908, and the American Locomobile was the fastest car in the world.

It seemed a stunning victory. But, as Elizabeth Janeway vividly recalls in *The Early Days of Automobiles,* this feat was only one proud moment in the whole rollicking story of the automobile in America. From the day the Duryea brothers won the first great horseless carriage race in 1895 at a speedy five miles an hour, to the super-streamlined cars of today, the story of the automobile has been one of trial and error, of laughter and disappointment, and of courageous men taking risks and tempting fortune.

In their Stanley Steamers, and their curved-dash Olds-mobiles the American people rumbled and bumped along. And as they traveled the shouts of "Get a horse!" grew fainter and fainter. The Age of the Automobile came into its own!

THE EARLY DAYS OF AUTOMOBILES

THE
EARLY DAYS OF
AUTOMOBILES

by ELIZABETH JANEWAY

Illustrated by HERTHA DEPPER

RANDOM HOUSE · NEW YORK

This title was originally catalogued by the Library of Congress as follows:

AUTOMOBILES—HISTORY

629.2   **Janeway, Elizabeth**
J   The Early days of automobiles; illus. by Hertha Depper.
Random House ©1956
     192p   illus   photos   (Landmark books)
     ". . . a history of the automobile: its invention, testing,
difficulties encountered, the performance of early automobiles,
the beginning of the industry, mass production, the influence of
the automobile in the changing American way of life—and the
dreamers, tinkerers, drivers, and skilled engineers who have had
a part in developing and perfecting the automobile."—*Booklist*
1 Automobile industry and trade   2 Automobiles—History
I Title

0406   629.2

Trade Ed.: ISBN: 0-394-80368-X   Lib. Ed.: ISBN: 0-394-90368-4

ACKNOWLEDGMENTS

I wish to acknowledge, with thanks, the kind permission granted for the use of quotations from the following sources: *Horseless Carriage Days* by Hiram Percy Maxim, Harper and Brothers, 1937; *Not So Long Ago* by Lloyd Morris, Random House, Inc., 1949; *The Pictorial History of the Automobile* by Philip Van Doren Stern, The Viking Press, Inc., 1953; *Those Bentley Days* by A. F. G. Hillstead, Faber and Faber, Ltd.; *Get a Horse!* by M. M. Musselman, J. B. Lippincott Company, Copyright, 1950, by M. M. Musselman; "Farewell, My Lovely!" by Lee Strout White, originally published in *The New Yorker*, 1936, and published in book form by G. P. Putnam's Sons under the title *Farewell to Model T* in 1936; *Kings of the Road* by Ken W. Purdy, Little, Brown and Co., 1952; *Free Air* by Sinclair Lewis, Harcourt, Brace and Company, 1919.

In addition, much interesting and useful material was found in the following publications: *Combustion on Wheels* by David L. Cohn, Houghton Mifflin Co., 1944; *Get a Horse!* by M. M. Musselman, J. B. Lippincott Co., 1954; *Fill 'er Up!* by Bellamy Partridge, McGraw-Hill Book Co.; *The Story of a Stanley Steamer* by George Woodbury, W. W. Norton & Co., Inc., 1950; *Westward Hoboes* by Winifred H. Dixon, Charles Scribner's Sons, 1921; *Sports Cars of the World* by Ralph Stein, Charles Scribner's Sons, 1952; *Treasury of Early Automobiles* (1950) and *Those Wonderful Old Automobiles* (1953), both by Floyd Clymer, McGraw-Hill Book Co. Mr. Clymer has also served the historian of the automobile well by re-issuing, himself, *The Story of the New York to Paris Race* (1951) published originally by the E. R. Thomas Company, and *The Saga of the Roaring Road* by Fred J. Wagner. In its issue of July 13, 1954, *Life Magazine* published a most amusing and colorful article on the New York-to-St. Louis tour, "Meet Me (Pop!) In (Crash!) St. Louis, (Squawk!) Louis" by Robert Wallace. Mr. Charles B. King's reminiscences of the 1895 Chicago race have been privately printed under the title, "Personal Sidelights of America's First Automobile Race."

The automobile manufacturers have kindly supplied material and responded to questions, and my thanks are due to them also, particularly to the Ford Motor Car Company and to the Cadillac Motor Car Division of General Motors.

I would like also to thank the numerous friends who suggested material to be used and recalled anecdotes of the early days of motoring, and to express my gratitude to Mike and Bill Janeway for their helpful editing and criticism of this book in manuscript.

Elizabeth Janeway

CONTENTS

THE EARLY DAYS OF AUTOMOBILES

1 THE GREAT RACE

THANKSGIVING DAY IN CHICAGO IN THE YEAR 1895 dawned on a city blanketed in snow. That meant fun for the children, you may be sure—coasting and snow fights and a trip in the family sleigh to Grandmother's house for turkey dinner. But it meant something very different to the men who were gathering at that early hour in Chicago's Jackson Park.

It meant something like a nightmare.

Thanksgiving Day was not a holiday to them. Thanksgiving Day was the day of the race.

What kind of a race? Anyone in Chicago could have told you. And whoever you asked would have added his own opinion too. Either this was the best joke and the biggest hoax since P. T. Barnum's circus exhibited his famous false "mermaid," or Chicago was about to see the opening of a new age of transportation. "Crackpot!" cried one side. "Stick-in-the-mud!" replied the other. There was only one thing they agreed on. This was going to be a great show, and no one was going to miss it.

No sir, no one was going to miss the great race of the horseless carriages—the first time in America when the new-fangled, gasoline-powered buggies were to compete.

But was there going to be a race? Eight inches of snow covered the course—the fifty-two miles from Jackson Park, Chicago, to Evanston in the suburbs and back again. The queer little contraptions that were going to try it looked like buggies that had mislaid old Dobbin. Could any of them manage to cover those fifty-two miles of slush and snowdrifts and rutted roads and potholes waiting to break an axle? Even their drivers, even their inventors, could not be sure. It was a worried group of men who worked feverishly in the dark early morning to get their vehicles ready, wrapping the narrow tires with clothesline to keep them from slipping in the snow.

The most worried of all was a young man who was neither inventor nor driver. Frederick Upham Adams was a reporter on the Chicago newspaper, *The Times-Herald*. But Fred Adams was something more. He was the man who had thought up the idea of the race. Over a year before he had read a report of a race for horseless carriages in France, from Paris to the city of Rouen. That race had been arranged by a French newspaper. Why shouldn't a Chicago newspaper offer Americans the chance to rival the French and Germans who had raced abroad?

So firmly did Fred Adams believe in his idea that he persuaded H. H. Kohlsaat, the owner of *The Times-Herald,* to offer prizes totaling $5,000. That was fine, but it was only the beginning of Adams' work. Where were the horseless carriages to come from? There were probably not more than ten in use in the whole United States at the beginning of 1895! That is what the other Chicago newspapers were asking, too, and not asking very politely.

Fred Adams set out to find the horseless carriages for his race. A series of articles told *Times-Herald* readers about the great future of the horseless carriage. Then, as questions about the race began to come in, Adams went off on a tour of the country. He visited such large firms as the Pope Manufacturing Company in Hartford, Connecticut, one of the leading makers of bicycles in the country. And he visited, too, those backyard workshops where eager young men were trying to turn their dreams into self-propelled reality.

Altogether, almost ninety applications to enter the race were received. They came from all over—from makers of engines and carriages and bicycles, and even from a manufacturer of wheel chairs and baby carriages. Most of the cars entered were to be driven by gasoline, steam or electricity. But more imaginative applicants stated that they planned to use carbonic acid, acetylene gas, or even the kind of steel springs that you wind up with a key to run a toy car today.

But of the ninety cars entered, only twelve showed up when the horseless carriages and their proud owners began to gather in Chicago And on that snowy Thanksgiving morning, only half—only six—were in Jackson Park ready to start. *The Times-Herald* had already postponed the race twice, in order to allow new entries to arrive. Fred Adams did not dare suggest another delay. He and his paper—and his boss, too—would be the laughingstock of Chicago if the race were put off again. Blizzard or no blizzard, the race must be run. It was up to six men and six motors to show America whether the horseless carriage was just a toy, or whether it was a rugged vehicle that could stand up to American distances, American weather and American roads.

Three of the six cars were of German make. All of these had gasoline engines designed by Karl Benz. There were two American electric cars among the starters—the Sturges and the Electrobat. The only American car driven by gasoline that crossed the starting line had been built by the Duryea brothers, Charles and Frank. A year of planning and two of practical testing on the roads around Springfield, Massachusetts, had gone into it. But neither the

Duryeas nor their automobile had faced a blizzard before.

The Duryea was the first car across the starting line at 8:55 A.M. Frank Duryea was driving with Arthur White beside him, for each car carried one passenger who was also a referee. Charles Duryea watched his brother go—and saw the two electrics and two of the Benz entries follow, and stall in the snow. The lightweight Duryea got through. However, enthusiastic spectators were pushing the stalled cars out of the snow despite the protests of the umpire-passengers that this was against the rules. There was no time to waste, Charles Duryea decided, and set off for the first official check point in the center of town, which each car had to pass.

In less than an hour Frank and the Duryea appeared, and the waiting crowd cheered. Charles drew a breath of relief, but he was leaving nothing to chance. Horseless carriages would someday transform America, of course. But in the meantime, Charles had decided a good team of horses might be useful. While Frank and the Duryea led the way to the future, Charles and a fast team clip-clopped along behind, just in case.

The first "just-in-case" happened before the Duryea got out of the heart of the city. In the report of the race that Charles wrote later he says calmly, "The steering apparatus broke." Now any car of today which had its "steering apparatus" broken would be laid up for days in a service station while mechanics replaced broken parts with duplicates from the manufacturer. But in 1895 the manufacturer of the Duryea car was the driver. Frank had the broken part off with a monkey wrench in a minute. After one look he said to Charles, "Find a blacksmith shop that's open."

Not so easy on Thanksgiving Day! But Charles' team of horses quickly covered the neighborhood and friendly folk directed him. Yes, there was a shop open. In less than an hour the "steering apparatus" was repaired, and off went Frank. But now he was no longer in the lead. The Benz that had been entered by R. H. Macy had splashed by. Frank gritted his teeth and set out to catch it. On he went through the slush. Ten minutes to eat a sandwich for lunch, and on again!

By now, word had come that some of the contestants had dropped out. One of the heavy Benz cars stalled so badly in the snow that it never even reached downtown Chicago. The Electrobat driver decided that he would never make the relay station where a new battery was waiting, and ran smartly into his garage. Harold Sturges, driving his own electric car, was more determined. He kept on until his battery did run down, and his horseless carriage had to be hitched to a horse and pulled into shelter. This was good news for Charles

Duryea as he went on to meet his brother again in the outskirts of the city.

But where was Frank? Charles, waiting at the official check point, grew worried. Hastily he whipped his team up and down the streets. At last, with a sigh of relief, he spied the Duryea standing at the curb. Squatting beside it, fanning a charcoal fire, was Frank. An electric connection to the spark that fired the gasoline had been jarred loose by the bad going. In this open-air workshop, like a gypsy blacksmith, Frank was heating the broken part until it could be bent into shape for the needed repair. Another hour was lost.

But it was the last bad delay. The Duryea had no more serious trouble. With the team of horses driving ahead to break the soft snow on the dirt road to Evanston, the little car plowed along. The weather had grown milder, and all of Chicago that had promised itself a chance to see the fun was out in strength.

Families in big sleighs, young men home from college driving fast horses in smart cutters, little boys "belly-whopping" alongside, football fans on their way to the game between Chicago and Michigan—all shouted and cheered. On went the Duryea. On went the two German cars left in the race, the Mueller Benz and the Macy Benz.

But the Macy Benz had been having its troubles. One of the rules of the race required that "each vehicle shall be provided with a trumpet, foghorn, or other . . . warning signal." That on the Macy car must have been too weak to command respect, for the driver, Jerry O'Connor, had begun the day by ramming a horsecar on Adams Street. Though Mr. O'Connor managed to pass the Duryea and keep ahead of it until Evanston was reached and the return trip was begun, his "steering apparatus" was in bad shape. The Duryea took the lead in Evanston and held it.

Perhaps O'Connor could have caught up if he had not had a second collision. But have it he did—and with none other than *The Times-Herald* reporter who was covering the race. That gentleman had just been tipped out of his sleigh as he crossed the tracks of the Milwaukee Railroad, and O'Connor drove into the driverless sleigh. Although O'Connor was going no more than four or five miles an hour, this second bump did not help his wobbly conveyance.

But O'Connor was a determined man. If the Benz was hard to steer, it was still willing to go. He set its wheels in the streetcar tracks and chugged on. Alas, fate was not through with him! In Rogers Park a horse-drawn hack provided material for a third collision. Unbelievably, O'Connor managed to get started again. But although he refused to give up, the engine of the Macy Benz was not so determined. It finally came to a stop and refused to be coaxed further.

Meanwhile the Duryea was chugging on to the finish line, with only the Benz entered and driven by Oscar Mueller to challenge it. But poor Mr. Mueller, worn out by cold and strain, collapsed. Charles B. King, the umpire, drove the Benz to the finish line with one hand while he supported the weary Mr. Mueller with the other. He finished just before nine o'clock, but Frank and the Duryea had rolled in at quarter past seven. The Duryea had won!

Next day *The Times-Herald* declared the race a tremendous success. Other Chicago papers still jeered. Oh yes, Frank Duryea had finished without breaking the rules. But he was only one out of the ninety who had entered. And his average speed was just over five miles an hour. Why, in the French races of 1894 and 1895 the winners had sped along at

Frank Duryea, wearing the bowler hat in the picture above, won the first automobile race in America in 1895. Note the steering apparatus on the Duryea automobile.

thirteen and fifteen miles an hour. The roads of France, maintained for hundreds of years, were smooth. Who in America would trust a flimsy horseless carriage to the rutted dirt tracks that made up most of the road system? No indeed, the horseless carriage had shown itself to be a failure. So said *The Chicago Tribune.*

But Charles and Frank Duryea went back to Springfield and back to work. Back to work, too, went Charles B. King who had almost finished his car, which was to be the first to run on the streets of Detroit. So did Elwood Haynes, whose car had been kept out of the race by an earlier accident. So did Hiram Maxim, one of the umpires, whose gasoline tricycle had frightened the president of the Pope Manufacturing Company, but had got Maxim a job there. So did all the other young men who were going to turn the horseless carriage into the automobile, and make America a nation on wheels.

2 TESTS, TRIALS AND TROUBLES

WHY DID THE AUTOMOBILE SUDDENLY APPEAR in the 1890s? It was not the invention of any one man; nor was it a new idea. A carriage that ran by itself had been a dream for well over a hundred years. In 1748 a Frenchman contrived one that ran by clockwork, and in 1825 an Englishman invented a contraption that was drawn by kites. In America, sails were tried. And for over fifty years locomotives had huffed and puffed themselves along tracks by steam power.

Still the automobile remained a dream, as fantastic as human flight. It was waiting, un-born, for two things. The first was something to make it go—a light engine that could carry its own fuel supply. The second was enough people who wanted to go somewhere.

In the ten years before the Chicago race, a gasoline engine appeared on the scene, crude and primitive, but of the same basic design that runs our cars today. And in those same ten years a lot of people had a taste of "going somewhere."

First, the engine. In 1885 a German named Gottlieb Daimler tried to modify an engine designed by another German named N. A. Otto. This was a stationary engine which ran on illuminating gas, the gas that lighted our homes before electric lights were invented. Daimler fixed the Otto engine so that it ran on gasoline. This meant that the stationary engine could become a movable engine. It could run on fuel that it could carry with it. That same year Karl Benz—the same Benz who designed the German cars that lost the Chicago race—hitched the engine up to a tricycle which rumbled over the cobblestones of Mannheim, Germany, under its own power.

Already, in America and elsewhere, steam had been used to propel heavy equipment for farm work or road repair. Then with the coming of electricity came the electric storage battery that could run a light vehicle for as much as twenty-five miles. So by 1895, three sources of power existed to take the place of the horse.

About ten years before, another invention had rocketed to popularity. With it came the first faint dawn of the day that would see America a nation on wheels. It was the safety bicycle.

Today the automobile has taken over our roads so completely that the bicycle is used largely by children. But this is not true anywhere else in the world. As close to the United States as Bermuda and the Caribbean Islands, the end of a working day sees a flight of homebound bicycles carrying adults back from work. And so it is all over Europe.

In the 1880s and '90s the bicycle became the adventurer's magic carpet. Young people went in for racing—"scorching," it was called. Handlebars were turned down and the serious scorcher rode almost flat out on his bike, like a jockey leaning forward along the neck of a race horse. Sober elders disapproved of scorchers, but often went in for touring themselves. Bicycle parties would set out to explore unknown country fifty miles from home for a week at a time, and anyone who had ridden one hundred miles in eighteen hours could join the Century Road Club of America and sport a gold bar for every hundred miles. Americans had "gone somewhere" before—west across the country as pioneers. Now "going somewhere" was becoming fun.

Hiram Maxim, the young man who had been an umpire at the Chicage race and was designing cars for the Pope Manufacturing Company, recalled in later years just when he had first dreamed of an automobile. He was riding a bicycle on a lonely road from Salem to Lynn, Massachusetts. It was a lovely summer night in 1892, and he had been calling upon a most attractive young lady in Salem.

Round and round went the wheels under him. Round and round went his feet, pumping the wheels along. What a wonderful thing it would be, thought young Mr. Maxim, if only a little engine attached to the bicycle could provide the power to turn the wheels. It shouldn't take much! As it was, he could cover the distance from Salem to Lynn on his bicycle in less than half the time that a horse and buggy needed. But with a little engine, and a proper carriage to attach it to . . . . Here Mr. Maxim fell into a daydream. As he wrote later, "Distances would be halved. Towns would be nearer together. More people would intermingle." Riding along that lonely road, his feet churning steadily, he saw all America changed by the magic of his idea.

Just four hundred years before, Columbus had set out to find new lands. We are apt to think of him as a lonely adventurer, and so he was in one way. But in another, he was one of many men of the fifteenth century who had suddenly been attracted by the idea of exploration. Just so, four hundred years later, many men in Europe and America were feeling the attraction of a new idea, the idea of a vehicle which would run by itself and free people to go where they chose when they chose. When Maxim's idea burst into his brain that summer night, he did not know that other men had dreamed of it, too, and were working toward it. Over and over again in the 1880s and 1890s, different men caught sight of the possibility of the automobile and tried to make the dream come true. Sometimes an idea can be just as catching as measles!

Who caught it first—that is, who built the first American car—is a question that has been disputed since at least 1895. Probably the credit should go to the Duryeas for the first gasoline-driven car. But Elwood Haynes of Kokomo, Indiana, always claimed that the Duryeas just hitched an engine to a buggy, while he built the first real car. Then there was Alexander Winton, who argued with Haynes for years over who built the first "production" car—car made to sell—and who made the first commercial sale. But then, what about Ransom Olds' first steam car, built in 1887? What about the drawings for a gasoline-propelled car that George Selden sent to the United States Patent Office in 1879?

No, it's impossible to give any one man credit for the automobile. And that is as it should be, for many, many men worked to perfect it.

Trouble plagued them. In the first place, they didn't know what they were doing and had to learn as they went along. When Hiram Maxim decided to build a gasoline engine, he knew nothing about the explosive power of gasoline. He bought half a pint from a suspicious paint-shop owner, and acquired also a brass cartridge case two and a half inches across and twelve inches deep. Into this he put one drop of gasoline. Then he plugged the open end of the cartridge case and rolled it around for a minute to let the gasoline evaporate and mix with the air. The next thing was to stand the cartridge case on end, unplug it and toss in a lighted match.

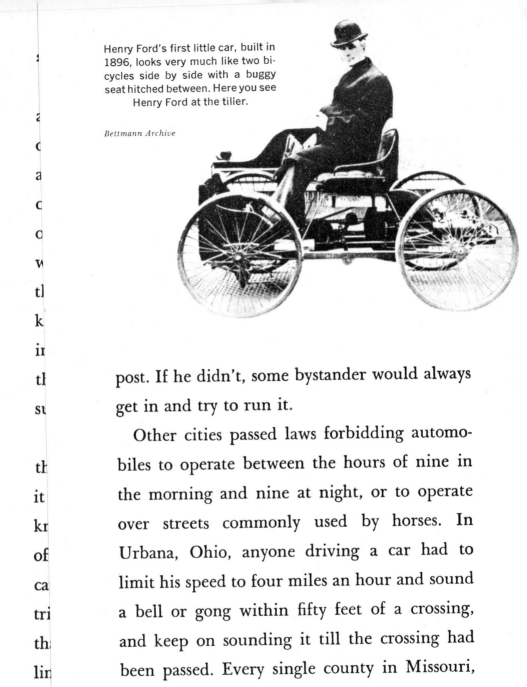

Henry Ford's first little car, built in 1896, looks very much like two bicycles side by side with a buggy seat hitched between. Here you see Henry Ford at the tiller.

Bettmann Archive

post. If he didn't, some bystander would always get in and try to run it.

Other cities passed laws forbidding automobiles to operate between the hours of nine in the morning and nine at night, or to operate over streets commonly used by horses. In Urbana, Ohio, anyone driving a car had to limit his speed to four miles an hour and sound a bell or gong within fifty feet of a crossing, and keep on sounding it till the crossing had been passed. Every single county in Missouri, except the city of St. Louis, made the motorist pay two dollars for the privilege of passing through. In St. Louis, he paid ten dollars. As for Mitchell, South Dakota, a city of ten thousand people, they passed just one law: no automobiles allowed within city limits at all!

On top of the human difficulties were the difficulties with another stubborn race—the horse. Every sensible, right-minded horse that met an automobile stood on his hind legs and had hysterics. One clever gentleman tried to calm the beasts by attaching a wooden horse's head and neck to the front of his horseless carriage. But if he thought he could fool the creatures, he was wrong. There might be human beings ready to say, for many years, that the automobile would never replace the horse; but it seemed as though horses knew better.

Another difficulty was the roads. In 1896 the French race, which now took place every year, was over a thousand miles long. In all of Amer-

American Automobile Assn. Photo

Cars drew to the side while frightened horses were coaxed by.

ica there were less than two hundred and fifty miles of good roads, outside of paved city streets. Springtime was "mud time," and everyone stayed home. Country roads could trap a wagon in mud so that even a team of big work horses couldn't pull it out. Streams rose as the snow melted, and when they didn't wash out bridges it was often because there weren't any bridges to wash out. In winter you crossed on the ice, when it was hard enough, and in summer you splashed across the stream at a shallow ford.

The roads we know today and the cars we know today had to be built together. So did the service stations. Hiram Maxim bought his first half-pint of gasoline in a paint and hardware store. He could have got it from a drug store, too, where it was sold for cleaning clothes. No one else carried it. The tire industry had to be created, too. When Alexander Winton built his first car, he had to make a special trip to the B. F. Goodrich Company and persuade the superintendent of the plant to make him a special set of big pneumatic tires. Only when he

Horses had a decided advantage over automobiles in the high water and swollen streams that flooded the roads.

American Automobile Assn. Photo

agreed to pay all the costs would the doubtful plant manager agree. Bodies for the first horseless carriages were built by carriage makers, and sometimes arrived with a socket on the dashboard for a whip with which to spur on the horse which wasn't there.

These were the difficulties which the pioneers of the horseless carriage faced. All they had on their side was a dream. It was a dream of freedom, of the chance for every man to go where he wanted when he wanted, for fun or for business, to work or to enjoy himself. It was a dream of an America that would no longer be a land of lonesome villages and farmhouses and little cities where the coming of a stranger was an event, where people used to go down to the railroad station for entertainment, just to watch the trains go through toward the great world they would never see. What the railroads began, the automobile carried on—the effort to make America "one nation, indivisible."

3 THE TOY THAT TURNED INTO A TOOL

THE FIRST PEOPLE WHO BOUGHT AUTOMOBILES in America were the rich and the fashionable. That's not surprising. The first automobiles were expensive. They were so hard to run that a chauffeur was a necessity. And he had to be not only a driver but also a mechanical specialist in what could go wrong with your car.

Almost anything could go wrong—and did. As you started out, you were never sure when, or if, you were going to arrive at your destination. No farmer, no hard-working country doctor, could waste his time tinkering with a temperamental engine, or patching the holes in tires that might go flat three times in ten miles. No, the horseless carriage was much too difficult for the average man.

Rich Americans first came in contact with automobiles in fashionable France. Except for the amazing Duryea, European cars of the 1890s were far ahead of American cars in design. Alas, the Duryea brothers found it impossible to work together. Frank went on to win other races in America and to take part in the London-Brighton run in England, where he made the best time, coming in ahead of a French Panhard-Levassor. But he and Charles quarreled over who was chiefly responsible for the success of the Duryea and parted company. While the men who were to make the American automobile industry the greatest in the world were still experimenting and learning, French

and German manufacturers were already turning out beautiful—and expensive—cars for sale
to the wealthy.

In 1897, Mrs. O. H. P. Belmont imported
the first French car to be seen in America. She
had it shipped to Newport, Rhode Island, that
most fashionable of all summer resorts, where
a millionaire's "cottage" might run to a hundred rooms. Of course Mrs. Belmont could not
drive very far in her car—just along paved
streets like Bellevue Avenue and Ocean Drive,
past the palatial "cottages" of her friends.
The roads around Newport were just as bad
as anywhere else. But Mrs. Belmont was much
more interested in turning the other leaders of
society green with envy, than in going somewhere. In this she certainly succeeded. What
did it matter that Mrs. John R. Drexel had
twenty-six different kinds of carriages in her
stable? She didn't have an automobile! Mrs.
Belmont was first again.

All fashionable Newport followed her lead. By 1899 anyone who was anyone owned a horseless carriage. At the end of the Newport season that year, Mrs. Belmont outdid herself once more. She gave a most spectacular automobile party. The grounds around her "cottage" had been laid out as an obstacle race for automobiles. There were wooden horses hitched to carriages. And dummy figures representing policemen, nursemaids and loafers had been placed along the course. The object of the contest was for Mrs. Belmont's friends to drive their cars in and out of the figures without knocking them down.

Mr. Belmont led the way with Mrs. Stuyvesant Fish in a runabout specially decorated for the occasion with yellow field flowers, topped by an arbor of cattails bearing a stuffed eagle. Mrs. Belmont and Mrs. J. W. Gerard came next in Mrs. Belmont's "golf-rig." It was covered with blue hydrangeas, and

Mrs. Belmont waved a whip made of hydrangeas and daisies. They were followed by a procession that included Colonel Jack Astor in a stanhope adorned with green and white clematis, and Mrs. John R. Drexel who had now added a horseless carriage to the twenty-six which still required horses.

It was a gala occasion. After the obstacle race had been run (with Mrs. Astor and Harry Lehr scoring zero by knocking down every single obstacle), the party set out on an hour's drive to Mrs. Belmont's country place. (One mansion at Newport was not enough for the lady.) An automobile ambulance full of mechanics and tools followed, to make any needed repairs. After dining and dancing, the procession returned to Newport, each car lit by little glow-lights until, as an excited journalist noted at the time, they looked like "a veritable pageant of fairy chariots."

Absurd? Of course it was. But it made a fine

story for the newspapers. And when the rich take up a fashion, some of the not-so-rich are always eager to try it, too, and get into the swim. On the other hand, the antics of Mrs. Belmont and her friends raised a very serious question about the horseless carriage. Was it just a toy for the rich to play with? Or did it have a part to play in American life? Could it be useful to ordinary folk in their everyday lives?

Ransom E. Olds and his "merry Oldsmobile" were the first to persuade America that the horseless carriage could be more than a fad for the wealthy. To Olds goes the credit of setting up Detroit's first automobile company. Detroit wasn't his original choice. He had tried to find backing in Newark, New Jersey. But though Newark was eager for new factories, none of its inhabitants was eager enough (crazy enough, was the way they put it) to trust their money to young Mr. Olds.

In this flower-decked "horseless carriage" Mrs. Astor and Harry Lehr took part in Mrs. Belmont's automobile race in 1899.

In Detroit, however, Olds met a retired copper millionaire with imagination and two sons who were automobile fans. The combination was lucky for Olds. He got his money, the boys got jobs, and Detroit got an automobile factory. The first Oldsmobile was not cheap. It was priced at $1,250. In 1900, when a steak dinner cost thirty-five cents, that sum would have bought a sound horse six times over. A French Renault car could be bought for $715. This first Oldsmobile did not sell.

So Olds determined to bring his price down. He built a little open runabout with a curved dashboard that could be sold for $650. And now fate took a hand. In March, 1901, a fire broke out in the Olds factory. Luckily the first and only little runabout was close to an open door. An excited workman tried to start it and failed, but the car was so light that he succeeded in pushing it out the door. It was the only thing that was saved from the fire. Even the plans for the big expensive cars had been burned. Olds had to make a low-priced car. It was all he had left to make. He had to make a car, not for the rich, but for ordinary everyday folks.

Ordinary everyday folks would want a car that was cheap. They would also want a car that was rugged, a car that wouldn't break down the minute it got off paved city streets. Olds decided to show them that his car was tough. The second New York Automobile Show was to be held in the fall. If the little Oldsmobile could make the run from Detroit to New York on its own, its toughness would be proved. What's more, newspaper stories would tell the world about it.

Working for Olds was a young automobile fan named Roy D. Chapin, who used to come back to the factory at night just to tinker with the cars he loved. (He held more important jobs when he was older—including United States Secretary of Commerce under President Hoover—but probably none that was so much fun.) One day Olds asked him how he would like to try driving the Oldsmobile runabout to New York. Chapin jumped at the chance.

Now to get the car ready! The factory hands and engineers went to work with a will. A special box was fitted to the rear of the runabout holding almost enough spare parts to build a new car. Chapin studied the maps of the country he had to cross, for there were no road numbers or route markers in those days to lead him along the dirt tracks he would have to follow. Just a week before the Automobile Show opened he started out. Though he wore a leather coat and motoring cap for protection against the weather in the little open car, a high starched collar encircled his neck, to celebrate the dignity of the occasion!

At the beginning things went fairly well. Chapin kept to the schedule he had planned as far as Syracuse, New York, though he had already found his box of spare parts very valuable. But at Syracuse it began to rain. Then it poured. Then came cloudbursts, and the roads washed out as dirt roads used to do. Old residents told Chapin he wouldn't get out of the city for a week—much too late for the opening of the Automobile Show. What was he to do?

In the nick of time, the worried Chapin learned of one road that hadn't—and wouldn't—disappear into mud and stones. It was the old towpath along the Erie Canal. Off he went in the little open runabout through the rain. For the next hundred and fifty miles he bounced along the towpath, meeting and overtaking furious mule drivers, who joined the barge captains in calling him everything under the sun they could think of—and they could think of a lot. At last he rolled into Albany and turned south on the old Post Road down to New York.

But fate hadn't finished with Chapin yet. A nasty bump in Hudson, New York, broke the car's axle, and he was held up for a day, working in a frenzy to fix the car to go on. Meanwhile Mr. Olds was waiting nervously for news in New York's old Waldorf-Astoria Hotel. At last Chapin wired that he was ready to go and would arrive the next day.

The next day passed, but where was Chapin? He was fighting his way down the Post Road in an obstacle race much worse than the one Mrs. Belmont had supplied for the entertainment of her guests. His obstacles were broken springs, punctures, ignition trouble, a broken feedline and—just a few blocks above the Waldorf Hotel—a bad skid that bounced the Oldsmobile into the curb. But the car was proving its mettle. As Chapin, covered with dirt and grease, pulled away from the curb, the crowd

Roy Chapin in the curved-dash Oldsmobile he drove from Detroit to New York in 1902. His average speed was 11 miles per hour.

that had gathered cheered him. On he went and pulled up to the front entrance of the Waldorf in a dream of glory.

Alas! It was a dream that the doorman of the elegant Waldorf did not share. To him, Chapin was no hero. He was a filthy and revolting object that could not be allowed to pass through the lobby of the hotel, horrifying the Waldorf's patrons. "Off with you!" cried the doorman, and Chapin ended his glorious adventure by sneaking around to a side door and riding up to Mr. Olds's room in a freight elevator.

Although the doorman at the Waldorf did not know it, Chapin and Olds had made history, and the Oldsmobile was the hit of the Automobile Show. A dealer signed up to take one thousand cars to be sold in and around New York. The great Chauncey M. Depew, president of the New York Central Railroad, bought an Oldsmobile and was photographed at the wheel—or rather, at the tiller, for the little runabout steered like a sailboat. The year after Chapin's drive, the Olds company made over two thousand cars. And the next year, in 1903, the Olds factory turned out one quarter of all the cars made in America. Olds had persuaded the public that the automobile had a real use. The days of the expensive, unreliable "horseless carriage" were ending. The age of the practical, useful automobile had begun.

4 COME FOR A SPIN!

WHAT WERE THEY LIKE, THOSE PIONEER CARS of the automobile age? Lots of Americans remember. Perhaps, if they lived in the country, some of them perched on a rail fence on a Sunday afternoon to watch the cars go by. Perhaps they remember the first car in town.

If this is so, it's more than likely that that wonderful first car was of a make you never heard of—a Winton, or a Thomas, or a Marmon, or even a Stanley Steamer. This is one of the ways that the early automobile age differed most greatly from today. Autos were made all over the country by small companies in small batches. More than two thousand different kinds of cars have been built in America since the turn of the century. Today, there are less than twenty different makes, all produced in great numbers by special machinery in huge factories.

Another difference is that the first automobiles were all open touring cars except for a very few luxurious electrics. Along about 1905 or 1906 cars began to be made with canvas tops that could be put up to cover the seats in bad weather. The automobile companies advertised that this was a simple job for one man; but it usually required the combined efforts of the whole family as the top was unfolded, metal struts pulled into position, nuts tightened, and the front bolted into place. It was not bolted to the windshield at first, for there wasn't any windshield. By 1909 or 1910 you could buy a windshield to attach yourself, but not until the teens of the century were windshields standard equipment.

Something else that early cars lacked was a self-starter. How did you start them? You cranked. Listen to M. M. Musselman, who learned to drive his father's big old Marmon when he was twelve:

"After you had set the spark lever at the third notch," (this gadget has disappeared, but the idea was to keep the engine from backfiring), "you went to the front of the car, bent over, put your shoulder to the radiator, grabbed the crank and turned the engine over twice while holding the choke wire. Then you released the choke, gathered together your full strength and spun the crank. As the first explosion came from the engine you dropped the crank and dashed for the wheel, where you advanced the spark a few notches and opened the throttle wide to race the engine until it warmed up.

"Of course, if you happened to forget and left the spark advanced when you cranked your car, the engine would backfire, knock you flat and probably break your arm into the bargain." Indeed, when the Model T Ford became so popular, there was a type of broken arm that doctors actually named the Ford Fracture!

The missing self-starter goes far to explain the popularity of the electric car. Electrics operated by power from big storage batteries. They started as simply as a flashlight goes on when you flick the switch—that is, they did unless the battery was dead. Only one lever was used to run them. Although their batteries had to be recharged with electricity every twenty-five miles, electric cars were perfect for ladies of fashion to use in paying their calls.

Not that all ladies were so timid even then! Mr. Musselman's mother, for instance, much preferred the enormous old Marmon. She solved the problem of how to start it by *standing* on the crank, clutching the thermometer on top of the radiator, and bouncing up and down on the crank until the motor caught. Once, alas, she forgot to retard the spark lever. The engine backfired and threw her like a bucking horse. Her cheek hit the thermometer and she acquired a black eye of startling size and color. But two weeks later she was cranking and driving the Marmon again.

In many ways the steam cars seemed more satisfactory to their devoted owners than the cranky gasoline autos of early days. They were very fast. A Stanley Steamer designed especially for racing did better than two miles a minute in 1906. And in 1907, it did better than three miles a minute. But this last record does not count, for the Stanley Rocket, racing on a Florida beach, hit an uneven spot and took off into the air like an airplane at almost two

Stanley Steamer alone, he managed to his horror to set it afire! Long sheets of orange flame licked up through the hood vents, and Mr. Woodbury leaped out of his adored Stanley in panic. But veteran Steamer men had assured him that if he turned off the fuel supply, opened the hood and waited, the fire would burn out in a couple of minutes. He did, and the fire burned out. The Stanleys had made the burner compartment of the old car almost completely fireproof.

To offset such embarrassing moments the steam car had great power. In those days, gasoline cars inched their way up hills with grinding and clashing of gears. The owner of a Model T Ford soon learned that trying to climb too steep a hill might mean that his engine gasped and died. That was because the first Model T's had no fuel pumps and relied on gravity to carry gasoline to the carburetor from the fuel tank. When the engine was higher than the fuel tank, the gasoline could not flow. As a result many a Model T owner put his car in reverse and backed up every tough hill that he came to. By doing that, he kept his chugging engine lower than the fuel tank and the gasoline could flow into the engine without difficulty. But the driver of a Stanley Steamer merely opened his throttle a trifle and climbed noiselessly past the laboring gas cars. Nor would his car explode, as many anxious folk thought. The Stanley twins had worried about that, too, and decided one day to see how much pressure one of their boilers could stand. They placed it in a pit in the ground, warned everyone away, and from a safe distance pumped steam into it. At two and a half times the normal operating pressure, they gave up. The boiler wouldn't explode because every boiler tube had sprung a leak and had become a safety valve.

The real trouble with the steam car was

getting it started. Just like a locomotive, it had to get up steam, and that took time. First you warmed up the burner jets and the pilot light with an acetylene torch. Then you ran in a little gasoline and burned that until you had got your burner hot enough to use the regular kerosene fuel. Finally you turned on your kerosene supply, and only then were you ready to begin heating the water in your boiler to make steam to run your car. Some experts claimed they could be ready to run in fifteen minutes, but half an hour was more like it for most people.

Now in the days when ladies like Mrs. Musselman were bouncing on the cranks of their cars to get them started and when the Ford Fracture was common, the chore of getting up steam didn't matter so much. But when the self-starter was invented, the steam car was doomed. In 1911 a self-starter appeared on some Cadillacs. It was the beginning of the end for the steam car. In 1918, after one of the Stanley twins had been killed in an accident, his brother sold the company. It did not finally close down until 1925, but the great days of the steamer were over.

But let's go back to 1905 and pretend that we're about to go for a drive. It will probably be a pleasant Sunday afternoon in summer. We won't take our open car out in the rain unless we have to, though it's possible to buy a kind of double-sized poncho with several holes for heads to come through which might keep us partly dry. As for winter driving, this is undertaken only by the most foolhardy. Antifreeze as we know it has never been heard of. Wrapping the cold engine in rags and pouring a kettle of boiling water over it may help to get it started. Putting a few drops of ether into each cylinder of the motor may help, too. But most people store their cars for winter out in

Automobile Manufacturers Assn. Photo
Early auto drivers had to be their own mechanics, for service stations and spare parts were unknown.

for help, for there are no service stations. We must make our own repairs. So in addition to a jack and a wrench, we carry files and punches, chisels and pliers, and such useful odds and ends as twine, rubber tubing, iron wire, and a short length of wood. Then there are special tools for removing wheels or gears, and a vulcanizing kit to prepare the rubber patches that we must use to cover puncture holes in tubes. We must have a pump to inflate our tires. And if an accident is too bad for Father and the boys to fix, there is the length of towline with which a farmer and a team can haul us to the nearest blacksmith shop.

Are we off to explore new territory? Then we must be sure that we have our Blue Book, the official guide put out by the newly formed American Automobile Association. Since road numbers and markers don't exist, the Blue Book gives us detailed lists of landmarks to look for. Mother or one of the older boys or girls must keep it open and read out to Father at the wheel such orders as, "Turn left at the stone church. Bear right at the fork by the iron watering trough. Follow the telegraph poles downhill to the trolley tracks and then left at the brick house. Leave the trolley tracks at the fork by the soldiers' monument."

If all goes well, we will get home before dark. But if a watering trough or a stone church has escaped Mother's eagle eye, or tire-patching has delayed us, we may find ourselves at dusk

A family takes a spin! The youngest passenger in this early automobile is Elizabeth Janeway, author of The Early Days of Automobiles.

lost in a strange countryside. Then we must stop and light our acetylene headlights. That does not mean flicking an electric switch. The acetylene gas that burns in the lights is usually made in a generator fastened to the running-board. Opening a valve allows water to drip slowly onto some calcium carbide. This produces acetylene gas, which flows along rubber pipes to the headlights. They are lighted with a match. Their glare will help us home—and the unpleasant smell that goes along with it will make us doubly glad to get there!

But in spite of all the nuisance, the number of cars in America continued to grow. By 1906 over a hundred thousand were in use. That doesn't seem like many today—but in 1896, there had been just sixteen cars in use in the whole country. For one thing, the overworked country doctor had begun to discover that a car would let him see more patients in a day than a horse and buggy could get him to in a week. In 1906 the Journal of the American Medical Association published a special section on automobiles for doctors. Here we can learn of the troubles and successes of men who were beginning to use automobiles, not for pleasure trips, but in their daily work.

Troubles they had aplenty. In Helena, Montana, Dr. C. B. Miller ended his first out-of-town call in a new car with carburetor trouble just as he got back to town. His gas leaked, and a short circuit suddenly produced showers of sparks. The whole car caught fire

—and there Dr. Miller's adventure would have ended in disaster, except that a neighbor was watering his lawn with a garden hose, and dashed over to put out the flames. Sadly Dr. Miller went back to his horse and buggy. Time after time he ordered a new carburetor. And time after time it broke down, and the doctor was dragged home by a team of horses. He swore off automobiles for a whole year. Finally

Many an automobile driver had to get oxen or horses to pull his "horseless carriage" out of the mud.

American Automobile Assn. Photo

he bought a new one and built a garage and workshop. Now that he was able to do his own repairs he found that he could keep his car running and see many more patients than ever before.

All across the country, from Boston to San Francisco, doctors were taking to the automobile. Like Dr. Miller, they often had trouble at first. Then they would put their medical training to work and strip down the machines that were plaguing them to learn their "anatomy." After a "thorough dissection" of his car, wrote Dr. Charles Muir, "I can get it started now before the crowd gathers round." No longer did he have to answer such helpful questions as "What's the matter, Mister? Won't it run?" or listen to advice to "Get a horse!" The automobile was beginning to show that it could be useful in the everyday chores of making a living.

first automobiles. It might take quite a while to get up a long steep hill behind a horse— sometimes everyone but the driver had to get out and walk—but there were hills that automobiles couldn't get up at all. *Their* drivers had to go miles around, out of their way. Another thing that plagued early motorists was dust from the dirt roads. A horse and buggy with its narrow tires didn't go fast enough to raise much, but every auto traveled in a dusty cloud that dirtied faces and clothes. There was an added advantage for the man driving a buggy. He knew that if he got a little bit lost on the unmarked roads, almost every horse could be trusted to find his way back to his own barn.

Makers of cars, then, had to sell the public more than automobiles. They had to sell the *idea* of owning and driving an automobile. Some of the ways they went about it seem quite odd to us.

Back in 1895, you remember, young Fred Adams decided to get people interested in horseless carriages by running the Chicago-to-Evanston race. Racing continued to be one of the most popular ways of interesting people in owning cars. Long before Henry Ford built the famous Model T, he constructed two big racing cars, the 999 and the Arrow. They developed 80 horsepower; this was in the days when most cars were ten or twelve horsepower jobs. To drive these demons, Ford, who had started his career as a bicycle mechanic, got hold of a famous bicycle racer, Barney Oldfield. Barney had never driven a car before. Ford gave him a week to learn, and then entered his 999 in a race, with Barney at the wheel. Barney had used his week of driving lessons well, for he took the lead at once and never lost it. He went on to become one of the most famous racing drivers of all time. He became so famous that for years policemen who stopped speeding

Here you see Henry Ford beside his famous racer 999 with Barney Old-field at the tiller. The 999 was built in 1902.

drivers would ask, "Who do you think you are, Barney Oldfield?"

Races were run all over the country, sometimes on specially built tracks, but often on ordinary roads. The best known and most popular of them all was the race for the Vanderbilt Cup, which was held each year on Long Island near New York City. Indeed, it grew too popular. In 1904 many people were angry when the first race was held for the huge silver cup that Mr. William K. Vanderbilt had offered.

Why, they asked, should daredevil drivers be allowed to take over public roads for racing? It might amuse rich automobile owners, but it would certainly inconvenience ordinary users of the roads. But to the horror of these indignant folks, and to the surprise of the rich, people of the New York area turned out by the thousands to watch the race and share in its thrills. The Vanderbilt Cup Races became like huge carnivals. Usually the course was about thirty miles long, and racers would make ten or eleven laps. But whatever the length of the course, thousands of people clustered around. The greatest crowds gathered at the most dangerous corners to watch such famous drivers as Lancia and Chevrolet skid around and shoot off in a cloud of dust.

By 1910 the crowds that turned out were too big for the police or even a regiment of soldiers to handle. In fact, before one race could begin, the tracks had to be cleared by turning hoses on the crowd to get them off the road. After 1910 the race was moved from Long Island. Later contests for the Vanderbilt Cup were run in Savannah, Georgia, Milwaukee, Wisconsin, and California.

Some idea of how fast the engineering of automobiles developed can be seen by the speed of the Vanderbilt racers. In 1905, just ten years after Frank Duryea won the Chicago race at an average speed of five miles an hour, a French Darracq won the Vanderbilt Cup at better than a mile a minute—sixty-one miles an hour.

In 1908 an American car with an American driver won the Vanderbilt Cup for the first time. This was George Robertson, at the wheel of a huge 120-horsepower Locomobile. Tens of thousands of people poured out of New York to see this race. It took a regiment of volunteers, plus large numbers of private detectives, to keep them from tearing down all the fences

George Robertson in a 120-horsepower Locomobile won the Vanderbilt
Cup Race in 1908.

to get a better view and swarming right across
the roads on which the drivers were speeding.

Robertson drove that Locomobile at an average speed of 64 miles an hour for a little over
four hours. He raced through a throng that
screamed with excitement as each car went by.
Trees were festooned with small boys who had
climbed up to get a good view and who some-
how never fell off under the wheels of the

racers. A driver knew that if he lost control he might kill twenty people as his car plowed into the crowd. The crowd knew it, too, but took it out in shrieking.

If the mob didn't help Robertson, neither did the other drivers. Every driver was supposed to pull over and let a faster car go by, but what racer likes to admit that anyone else is faster? Robertson, with his mechanic riding beside him, roared up behind a Thomas Flyer, but neither his horn nor his yells could make the Thomas move out of the center of the narrow road. Something had to be done. Holding the wheel with one hand, Robertson grabbed his mechanic's overalls with the other, and that gentleman stood up in the speeding Locomobile and heaved a wrench at the Thomas! There was a loud clang as the heavy wrench made contact with the gas tank of the Thomas, and its driver yielded the center of the road with no further delay.

Four hours at better than a mile a minute is not easy driving, even today, and Robertson's Locomobile had the opposite of what modern advertisements call "fingertip control."

"I was thick in the shoulders in those days," Robertson said. "You had to be. The steering ratio was almost one-to-one and it took an ox to turn the wheel. There were 110 pounds of pressure on the clutch pedal and after you'd pushed that down every minute or so for four and a half hours you walked sideways."

Into the last lap came the Locomobile, leading its rivals by four and a half minutes. All along the course eager fans leaned out to see Robertson smoke down the road to the first American victory. Then a universal groan went up. The Locomobile had pulled into its repair pit, and those in the know passed the word that in its last race it had been plagued by tire trouble. One minute, two minutes, three minutes passed as the crowd waited with mounting

tension. Then out on the road plunged Robertson and his monster.

Now he really had to travel to make up for
lost time. On the last lap around the course,
he crossed the humped bridge at Meadowbrook
so fast that the car took off from its crest and
was airborne for almost as long as the Wrights'
first flight at Kittyhawk. When his speed was
clocked, it was found that he'd covered the last
fourteen miles at 102 miles an hour!

That Locomobile is still running today,
owned by an old car fan who keeps it in as fine
shape as when it entered the 1908 race. And
only a few years ago, George Robertson drove it
again. He and the Locomobile entered a race
for vintage automobiles held at Carmel, New
York. It's good to be able to report that the two
wonderful old-timers won again.

The year 1908 witnessed another race that
excited people as much as the Vanderbilt Cup.
That was the remarkable contest whose starting

line was in New York City—and whose finish was in Paris, France. New York to Paris by car, not by ship! How could it be done?

The answer is not that they swam the Atlantic. The American Thomas Flyer, the Italian Zust and the German Protos that finished went around the world to do it. They crossed the United States, went by ship to Japan, drove across that country, took ship again to Vladivostok, drove across Siberia and European Russia to Moscow, thence to Berlin and on to Paris. The race began on February 12th and ended late in July.

In those months the drivers and mechanics met the most awful driving conditions that can be imagined. They left New York in a snowstorm and had blizzards all the way to Chicago. "We're doing very well," one of the foreign drivers wrote home. "We dig faster every day." The Americans in the Thomas Flyer, George Schuster and Montague Roberts with George

Miller as chief mechanic, were no better off than the foreigners. One day it took them fourteen hours to cover seven miles in the supposedly civilized eastern United States.

After Chicago the racers ran out of blizzards and into mud. The mud froze over at night, and in the morning the rutted roads made the drivers feel they were bouncing across a plowed field. Then, as the sun grew warmer, the ruts thawed and coated the cars with mud as they wallowed through. The crew of the Thomas Flyer learned to borrow a hose from the local fire department, when they stopped for the night, and wash their car down with it. It was the only way they could get rid of the sticky mud.

The people who planned the race had wanted the contestants to go from the West Coast to Alaska, and drive the wilderness roads there. The Thomas Flyer tried. Its crew received a magnificent welcome when they arrived by ship at the dock at Valdez, Alaska. Out of a population of 787, all but one came to see the first car ever to reach Alaska. The 787th stayed behind to blow the whistle at the steam laundry when the brass band struck up. But a trip in a sleigh to explore the roads outside Valdez convinced the Thomas crew that Alaska was not yet ready for the automobile age. Back to Seattle, Washington, they went by ship, and on to Japan.

Japanese roads presented a new difficulty. Where American roads were built for horse-and-buggy travel, most of the tracks of Japan were intended to be used by nothing bigger than rickshaws, the little two-wheeled carts pulled by manpower. Some were so narrow that a car couldn't use them at all. Even on the widest roads, turning a corner might mean backing up and inching forward two or three times before the wheels could be cramped around. And on mountain roads where an abyss yawned on one side of the road, the crew picked the Thomas up and carried it around the curves.

But at last the Thomas inched its way across Japan and went on to Vladivostok, the eastern-most seaport of Siberia. Here its crew ran into a new obstacle. Other cars had arrived earlier, for their drivers had not tried to make the impossible trip through Alaska. The canny crew of one car had decided to try to hold back the other contestants by buying up all the gasoline supply.

What were the Americans to do? Wait for a supply of fuel to be shipped in from Japan? Fortunately a number of Americans were living in Vladivostok then. They got together and appealed to the owners of all the motorboats in the city for help. Contributions of a gallon of gasoline here and two or three there soon mounted up, and the Thomas was able to go on.

The roads had been bad before. In Siberia,

there were stretches of miles where there were no roads at all—only trackless plains where the wild nomadic horsemen pastured their herds as they had done in the days of Genghis Khan. As the frozen earth thawed out with the advance of spring, the Thomas sank axle-deep into it. Only one trail crossed the Siberian tundra, and that was the track of the Trans-Siberian Railroad.

The dogged Americans in the Thomas found themselves "playing train" in dead earnest. The car was pushed and pulled onto the railroad ties between the broad-gauged Russian tracks. Then it began some hundreds of miles of bumping across the ties—a trip that made "the rocky road to Dublin" seem smooth. For unless a speed of at least 25 miles an hour was kept up, the wheels of the car were apt to stick be· tween the ties. It was like driving over a succession of man-made potholes. Added to this was the knowledge that the express from St.

Petersburg might thunder down the one-track line at any moment.

At last the ground dried out enough for the Thomas to say good-by to the railroad tracks and set off across the plains, guided by compass readings or the sign-language directions of the nomads. The German Protos was ahead, but Americans in the Thomas were determined to catch it. But alas, fate had other plans. A river ferry carrying the Thomas sank with it aboard. The car was salvaged successfully, but soon after that it was half-swallowed in a swamp. In straining to get out, sections of teeth were broken off the driving gear. The local black-smith, faced with the first automobile he had ever seen, did his best. But progress was slow until more repairs could be made as the Thomas approached European Russia.

The Americans made fine time now, except for the usual problems of hysterical horses, for Russian steeds did not care for automobiles any more than American ones did. For some reason, too, the peasants of European Russia found the Americans' sign language harder to understand than had the Siberian nomads. But the gap between the Thomas and the leading Protos was closing slowly. Not in time, though. The Thomas reached Paris on July 30th and found that the Protos had come in four days before.

However, nothing could stop the celebration

This Thomas Flyer won the New York-to-Paris race in 1908. The car is now on display in Southampton, N.Y.

Long Island Automotive Museum Photo

that greeted the Americans. And when the race committee took into account the time that the Thomas had spent on its trip to Alaska, it was seen that the actual driving time of the Americans was shorter by far, and the Thomas was declared the winner. The Paris crowds cheered generously, though all three French entries had had to drop out, and the Round-the-World Race passed into history as a feat that has never been surpassed.

What was the use of it? What was the use of the records set and broken in the Vanderbilt Cup Races, and later at the Indianapolis Speedway?

There was a real use. These contests were not just stunts. They tested cars as they could be tested no other way. The ability of a car to hold the road on curves, to stand up reliably to bad roads, to keep its driver safe even when he risked danger—all these things were tested in the races. Because of the lessons learned in racing, cars were constantly improved.

The well-known writer, Bellamy Partridge, has been an enthusiastic automobile fan since he bought one of the first Ramblers, in the early years of the century. Here is a list that he has made of the improvements that the automobile driver owes to racing:

Streamlining

Knee action

Four-wheel brakes

Balanced crankshafts

Improved bearings

Lower radiators

High-speed engines

Better shock absorbers

Aluminum pistons

Longer lasting sparkplugs

In addition, he points out balloon tires were first proved sound and safe in racing. And it was at the Indianapolis Speedway in 1911 that racing driver Ray Harroun first used a rear-view mirror to see behind himself at 90 miles an hour. The frightful driving conditions that the Thomas met and overcame in Siberia were only slightly worse than those Americans drivers faced in our own West, and even in parts of the East. Every bit of hard driving experience was put to good use by the men who made cars, and thousands of adventurous motorists contributed.

6 HENRY FORD WINS A FIGHT

As THE TWENTIETH CENTURY GREW OLDER, THE
automobile industry grew up. In 1906, there
had been a hundred thousand cars in use in the
United States. Five years later, in just the one
year of 1911, more than a hundred thousand
passenger cars and trucks were made. Indeed,
1911 was one of the greatest years the automobile industry has ever seen, a year full of events
that were to change the future.

For the racing fan, 1911 saw the first of the famous Memorial Day races at the Indianapolis Speedway, races which still draw crowds in the hundreds of thousands each year. Ray Harroun won the 1911 race, with the help of his rear-view mirror. His first words to the crowd of photographers who surrounded him as he rolled to a stop were, "Give me something to eat!"

An even more famous name is that of one of the relief drivers at Indianapolis in 1911—Eddie Rickenbacker. His days as a racing driver prepared him to become one of America's air aces in World War I.

In 1911, too, a practical and efficient self-starter appeared on a car. This was the brain child of Charles F. Kettering, one of the greatest inventors of the auto industry. For years eager and ambitious men had tried to find some way to end the nuisance that went with cranking a car. Without a self-starter, few women would dare drive anything but the slow, short-distance electric cars. Besides the nuisance, there was a real danger, too. The Ford Fracture was bad enough—that broken wrist that could be caused when an engine backfired as it was being cranked. But too often a forgetful driver would leave a car in gear. Then, when he cranked it and the engine caught, the monster would roll forward and run him down.

A self-starter was certainly needed. But how was it to be made to work? Where was the power to come from which would turn the engine over? Acetylene gas was tried and did not work. Neither did springs nor compressed air.

Kettering tried electricity. Since storage batteries were already being used to run electric automobiles, it is hard now to see why the idea of using one to start an engine was jeered at. Nevertheless, it was ridiculed by men who thought that because something had never been done it *could* never be done.

But Kettering found a man who believed in

his idea—Henry Leland of General Motors. Leland was deeply interested, for one of his old friends had been badly injured cranking a car, and the car was one of the Cadillacs that Leland's company made. Leland had vowed that a workable self-starter must be found. He ordered four thousand of Kettering's self-starters—an order so big, in those days, that Kettering had trouble filling it.

Leland had trouble, too. Other men in General Motors, without Leland's imagination and technical knowledge, declared that he was going to ruin the company by tying up so much money in a gadget that couldn't possibly work. These men brought in three well-known electrical engineers, and each predicted that Kettering's self-starter would not be practical. "Wait and see," said Leland and Kettering, and on a cold February day they invited the doubters to a test. With his white beard, Leland looked rather like Santa Claus testing some

strange 80-reindeer-power sleigh as he climbed
into the seat of the first self-starting Cadillac.
As his doubtful friends watched, he turned the
switch and pressed the button. At once, the
engine roared into life! The self-starter had
arrived. As it came into use, the gasoline car
slowly drove the steamers and the electrics off
the scene, for now the gasoline car could be
everyone's car.

Another event of 1911 was the founding of
the Chevrolet Company, to sell a light, low-
priced car named after the famous racing driver,
Louis Chevrolet. By 1911, it was clear that
Americans wanted a low-priced car. Ransom
Olds had started the trend with his little runabout. Henry Ford's Model T had shown that
it was more than just a flash in the pan. Now
Chevrolet was out to challenge him.

But it was not a challenge to Ford that made
the biggest news in 1911. It was a victory for
him. For in 1911 Henry Ford won the biggest,

most important dispute within the automobile industry. This was the lawsuit about the Selden Patent. It was a dispute in which Ford was on one side—and all the big automobile companies were on the other—a dispute that might have put Ford completely out of business if he had lost.

To understand it, we'll have to go back quite a bit—back past the very earliest days of the horseless carriage to the 1870s when the carriage-that-ran-by-itself was just a dream in the heads of various "crackpots." That was when George B. Selden, a patent attorney of Rochester, New York, applied for a patent on "a gasoline motor as the propelling force of a road vehicle, and upon the vehicle as a whole."

Webster's Dictionary describes a patent as "A writing securing to an inventor, for a term of years, the exclusive right to make, use and sell his invention." George B. Selden was applying to the United States Patent Office in

Washington for the right to be the only person in the United States allowed to make and sell "a road vehicle" driven by a gasoline motor.

In the United States, a patent right lasts for 17 years. By the end of that time, our government has decided, the inventor should have obtained enough money from his exclusive right to make and sell his invention to pay him back for his idea and for the time and effort he spent in developing it. If George B. Selden had secured his patent in 1879 when he first applied for it, it would have run out in 1896, when the horseless carriage was just beginning to come into use. He would have made very little money from it.

Selden was smart enough to see that his idea for a gasoline-driven road vehicle was well ahead of its time. He was a patent lawyer himself, however, and he knew how to keep his application in force without actually getting a patent. He did this by sending to the Patent

Office a stream of improvements and changes in his original idea, but not taking the patent out. And of course, being a patent lawyer, he kept an eye on *other* patent applications too. Meanwhile, he waited for the rest of the world to catch up with him, and for the automobile to come closer to practical use.

For sixteen years Selden kept his application pending. Finally, in 1895, when European cars were in production and American tinkerers were turning out their first models, his patent was granted. Selden had never built an automobile himself although he had tried to get money to make and sell a car. But he made the mistake of saying to his possible backers that someday automobiles would be as common as horse-drawn carriages. Shocked at this crazy claim, the men who had been thinking about putting money into his project gave it up.

But Selden took out his patent anyway and in the late 1890s a group of wealthy businessmen, who had invested money in running electric trolley-car lines, decided that electric taxicabs might be a money-making idea. They investigated the auto business thoroughly and decided that electric cars were the only practical ones. On the other hand, they didn't want to be bothered by competition from the makers of gasoline cars, so they bought from Selden his exclusive right to build such vehicles under his patent.

To their astonishment, this group of hardheaded businessmen found that gasoline cars were selling better than electrics, and improving fast. The Selden patent had not seemed very important when they bought it. By 1903, things were different. The automobile industry was beginning to grow, and gasoline cars were the coming thing.

Well, the holders of the Selden patent decided, they knew what to do about that. They set up the Association of Licensed Automobile

Manufacturers. Everyone in America who wanted to make cars had to come to the ALAM and apply for a license. If they didn't, said the patent holders, they could be sued for breaking the law by making cars without the right to do so. Ten manufacturers joined at once. It was easier, they felt, to pay the ALAM a small amount for each car they built than to take the chance of being sued for ignoring the exclusive right, bought from George Selden by the ALAM, to manufacture automobiles. Eventually every maker of cars, of any size at all, joined the Association of Licensed Automobile Manufacturers. That is, every maker except one.

Through these years of the late 1890s and the early 1900s, Henry Ford had been trying to set up an automobile company. So had hundreds of other young men, of course. Many of them, like Ford, were farm boys who hated the back-breaking work of old-fashioned farms without machinery and loved to tinker with engines.

There was nothing to show that Ford was any different from the others who tried and failed. He became a bicycle mechanic, and his first little car, built in 1896, looks very much like two bicycles side by side, with a buggy seat hitched between. Then he got a job as an engineer for an electric power company, and went on building cars in his spare time. But he was told firmly that an engineer with an electric company should not be interested in cars that used gasoline. When he refused to give up his hobby, he was fired.

He tried to form his own company to build cars, and a few were produced. But Ford made a mistake—a big one, and one that taught him a lesson. He wanted to build powerful, expensive racing cars. He and his friends did not have the money to compete with the companies that were already building such cars, and his company failed.

On his own again, Ford decided that though a big racing car was not a sensible thing to try to sell, a successful racer might make his name well known, and give him a reputation. It was then, in 1902, that he built the 999 and found Barney Oldfield to drive it. Years later, Barney used to say, "Henry Ford and I made each other. But I did a better job than he did." He was right. For it was after Barney had driven 999 smoking down the track to beat Alexander Winton's Bullet by half a mile that Ford got his chance. A wealthy Detroit coal dealer, Alexander Y. Malcolmson, decided that there was money to be made in automobiles and that Ford was the man to head his company.

In 1903, then, the Ford Motor Company was set up, with $28,000 in actual cash to begin work. The people who put in these thousands lived to receive millions in return, for the Ford

Motor Company was to succeed beyond even Henry Ford's wildest dreams. From 1916 to 1926 half of all the cars manufactured in America were Fords.

These were the famous Model T's, the Tin Lizzies of song and story. They were not the very first Fords, for Henry Ford had had a hankering to build a big, powerful car. He had tried out his six-cylinder Model K, selling for $2,500, and also a small cheap four-cylinder car at the same time. The results were surprising and convincing. It was the small cheap car that made money, for it was the small cheap car that ordinary people could afford to buy, and by this time, they wanted cars. Horse-and-buggy days were gone forever.

So Henry Ford made his famous announcement. From now on his factory was going to build just one type of car and one alone. It would be cheap enough to compete with the horse and buggy, sturdy enough to run on the back roads of rural America, and simple enough for almost anyone to be able to repair as well as to run. A plain car for plain people, it would carry no expensive gadgets, and would not try to be stylish. Such things were luxuries for the rich. As for color, Mr. Ford was reported to have said, "Any customer can have a car painted any color he wants, so long as it is black."

Thus, in October, 1908, the Model T was born. At once the shiny black boxes on wheels began to sell like hot cakes. It seemed as though all America had been waiting for the Model T. Henry Ford, the boy from the farm, the former bicycle mechanic, had the car that the farmers and the tinkerers with machines wanted. The only thing he *didn't* have was a license under the Selden patent.

Instead, he had a lawsuit. The Association of Licensed Automobile Manufacturers thundered that Henry Ford was breaking the law every time he built a car without their permission. Worse still, everyone who bought a Ford was breaking the law, too, and might be sued. And in 1909 the holders of the Selden patent won their case in court.

That didn't stop Henry Ford. At once, he appealed to a higher court, the United States Court of Appeals, which ranks just under the Supreme Court. Had he the right, he wanted to know, to go on making and selling the low-priced cars that ordinary Americans wanted? By this time, the ALAM was threatening to put him out of business if they won the appeal. They would not, they said, grant him a license even if he agreed to pay the fee they asked. And they were threatening his customers, too.

His customers were loyal. Henry Ford, they felt, was not only building the kind of car that most people wanted and could afford. He was also fighting the power and the threats of the rich men who wanted to keep the automobile industry in their own hands. He was on the side of the common people against Big Business. In 1909, the country felt itself very much threatened by secret agreements among big businessmen, agreements to keep prices high and to make unfair profits. President Theodore Roosevelt had fought these Big Business combinations. And in Henry Ford, as in Teddy Roosevelt, many people felt they had a champion. When Ford offered to insure everyone who bought one of his cars against losing money in the lawsuit over the Selden patent, only fifty people out of eighteen thousand asked for such a bond. They believed in Henry Ford.

For two years, though, no one could be sure that Ford and his company would not be wiped out. Even his huge new plant at Highland Park, just north of Detroit, might be forced to stop work almost as soon as it had begun. Hundreds of different makes of cars had already come and gone. Was the Ford to be another? Would the Model T disappear from the American scene and the Ford name become another in that list of vanished cars? Would it be as forgotten as the Winton, the Pope-Hartford, the Chalmers, the Stoddard-Dayton, or that fantastic car of 1911, the Octo-auto which had eight wheels?

In 1911 the United States Court of Appeals gave its answer. Henry Ford was declared "Not Guilty." His automobile was not using the Brayton engine which Selden used. Indeed no automobile maker was using Brayton engines so no one was infringing on the Selden patent. The technical difference is that Selden's engine used only two strokes of the piston in the cylinder (one up, one down) to deliver power to the wheels of the car and to clear the burned gas out of the cylinder. The Otto engine, which developed into today's automobile engine, uses four strokes of the piston (two up, two down). This is more efficient because the exhaust stroke to clear out the burned gas is separated from the stroke of the piston which delivers the power to move the car. No one, said the Judges of the Court of Appeals, had a patent on it. Henry Ford was as free to use it as he was to use that even more wonderful invention —the wheel.

For Ford, it was a triumph. For the American people, it meant that the low-priced car, the car that almost every family could own, was here to stay.

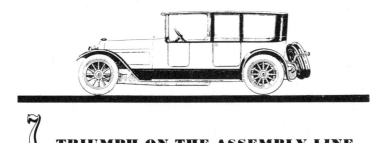

7 TRIUMPH ON THE ASSEMBLY LINE

FORD'S TRIUMPH, LIKE ALL SUCCESSES, BROUGHT problems with it. Before they were solved—solved not only by the Ford Company, but by other auto makers, too—the old-fashioned ways of building cars had been changed from stem to stern. The kind of factory that Ford developed, and the methods used in it, were taken over by the manufacturers of many other things. When the principle of producing parts and assembling cars in a long line was worked out by Ford, an idea almost as important as the automobile itself had come into being.

Ford wanted to build cheap, simple cars. People wanted to buy them. How was he going to make enough cars, cheaply enough, to supply all his customers?

The way *not* to make a cheap, simple car is the way that the first automobiles were built, and the way that many fine, expensive foreign cars have always been built. You might think that the best way to start a successful auto company would be to begin by making a few cars at a time in a small plant, without putting a lot of money into big special machines. You would be dead wrong.

In 1919, for instance, an English engineer named W. O. Bentley decided to form a company to build a car he had designed himself. It was an excellent car, for Mr. Bentley had had a great deal of experience designing fine engines. When he had finished the working drawings of his engine, he had the necessary parts specially made by various machine shops and hired a skilled mechanic to put them together. This mechanic, says the historian of the Bentley Company, "worked with the precision of a watchmaker."

Of course, when you are building the first model of something new, as an experiment, you must have skilled, precise mechanical work. The big auto companies still build the experimental models of future cars this way. But Bentley wanted to go on doing it. His car, he had decided, was to be "hand-built." Each engine was to be inspected and tested within an inch of its life, and the price of the car was the least important thing about it.

Bentley began on such a small scale that he had no factory at all—only some offices in an old building in the center of London. As a result, the first test of his new engine was almost its last. No exhaust, to silence the engine's explosions, had been fitted; and when the motor woke into sputtering life, it made an awful din. Within five minutes a furious nurse arrived from a small private hospital next door, threatening to call the police. The first test of the Bentley engine came to a hasty end.

Still, the first Bentley car was put together and shown at the London Auto Show. It was a beautiful piece of work and was much admired. But it couldn't be sold. It was not just the first Bentley. It was the only Bentley.

But little by little, Bentley began making cars in a brick shed outside London. They were built one at a time, two at a time, with the parts made elsewhere and carefully fitted together by hand. Isn't that the simplest, easiest way to do it? The answer is, "Look what happened to the price of the Bentley." The plan had been to sell it for 750 English pounds, which at that time amounted to about $3,750. That was not cheap. Before the first regular (not experimental) Bentley reached its owner, the price had climbed to $5,250. And this was not for a finished car. It was for a stripped-down chassis without headlights, spare tire, fenders or runningboard. To put a special body on the chassis might run over $2,000 more. The beautiful hand-built Bentley had priced itself right out of reach. Only a handful of people could afford it.

Aside from its price, there was nothing wrong with the Bentley and everything right with it. It was a magnificent car. Year after year, Bentleys won the most famous European road race, the 24-hour Grand Prix of Endurance at Le Mans, France. Four Bentleys entered the Le Mans race in 1929. They finished in first, second, third and fourth place. Said the English magazine, *The Motor,* "The victorious Bentleys came into the finish unhurried, dignified, superb, disposed in line ahead like a squadron of battleships."

But two years later, the company had failed. For 1929 also saw the end of the easy boom times of the 1920s. With the crash of the stock market, many people lost money. The handful of people who could afford Bentleys grew smaller and smaller. Bentley had aimed at building a car that would be "the plaything of the wealthy." A. F. C. Hillstead, former sales-manager of the company, who writes of *Those Bentley Days,* tells us that Bentley had wanted his car "to take pride of place in the stables of those eastern potentates who thought nothing of owning twenty or thirty motorcars."

As Henry Ford had found out thirty years before, such an aim is a short cut to failure, no matter how well a car is built, from the 999 to the beautiful last Bentley. The Bentley Company found it out too late. "If only," writes Mr. Hillstead, "we could have marketed a sporting four-seater at 750 pounds ($3,750) complete, or better still, had a popular model that would have appealed to the ordinary motorist, what a different story might have been told." But what a big "If" that is!

The way Americans found the answer to that "If" was by what we call "mass production methods." In the automobile industry that means, first of all, turning out a lot of cars, not just a few. Because a lot of cars are to be made, they must be made in a new way. Skilled mechanics can't be used to fit the parts together by hand, test them, and adjust them if they don't quite fit. That takes too long, and it costs too much.

In mass production, machinery must take over for the skilled mechanic. The parts that go together to make a finished car must fit together at once, without being specially adjusted. Each cylinder head must be like every other cylinder head to a tiny fraction of an inch. Each valve, each spark plug, must be exactly like its brother. The great presses that stamp fenders and parts of the body from sheets of steel must make each fender the twin of those made before and after it. Every part must fit the parts next to it in any car of the same model, so that one can be changed for another without special fitting and adjusting.

The idea of such "interchangeable parts" was not new to American industry when automobiles began to be built. Colonel Colt had made his Colt revolvers this way, and Eli Whitney had hit upon it in building the cotton gin.

The use of interchangeable parts was no secret that Americans wanted to keep to themselves, either. Back in 1908 Henry Leland of the Cadillac Company, who had worked at the Colt Arms Factory, went to great pains to show English auto makers the value of interchangeable parts. Leland was sure that the Cadillac was as fine a car as could be built. Still, foreign "hand-built" cars appealed to many wealthy people. Leland hoped to get some of these

On the first Ford assembly lines, which began work in 1914, the body of the car was dropped onto the chassis as it came along.

Today new cars come off the assembly line at more than one a minute. The bare frame becomes a finished car in ninety minutes.

people as customers by showing what his machine-built Cadillacs, with their interchangeable parts, could do.

To prove his point, he turned over three cars from the Cadillac agency in London to the Royal Automobile Club. The Cadillacs were taken to the big auto-testing grounds and race track at Brooklands, England. Under the watchful eyes of English officials, they were taken completely to pieces. In a few hours' time the three cars had been turned into a great heap of auto parts. "Jumble them up together!" Leland had told his men, and soon those three Cadillacs were as scrambled as any eggs have ever been. No one could tell from which car any one part had come.

Now the heap of parts was sorted into three. From each of these piles eighty-nine pieces were taken at random and replaced by new parts from the Cadillac warehouse. Only then did the Cadillac mechanics begin to put the three cars together again. They were allowed to use only the simplest tools—wrenches, hammers, screwdrivers and pliers. No special equipment with which to adjust one part to fit another was allowed.

Slowly the three heaps of parts turned once more into three Cadillacs. But whether parts that had gone together in the first place were fitted together again at the end, no one knew. What's more, no one had to care, for all the parts *did* fit together. They were truly interchangeable, for they had certainly been interchanged. Proudly the mechanics turned over the finished cars to Royal Automobile Club drivers, and watched them taken out on the Brooklands track for testing. Each Cadillac was driven five hundred miles by English drivers, and each one finished the run with a perfect score. For this performance Cadillac won the coveted Dewar Trophy, presented by the Automobile Club of London. The machine-built car had proved itself the equal of the hand-built car.

The first of our "mass-production methods," then, is that the parts that are turned out must be interchangeable. How do they get that way? By another "mass-production method"—the use of special machinery. In today's auto factories you will find regiments of drills, presses and lathes. Each is so enormous and complicated that it looks as if it could do almost anything. But it doesn't do "almost anything." It does just exactly the same thing over and over and over again, doing it accurately to hundredths, and sometimes thousandths, of an inch.

Here, for instance, in Ford's huge River Rouge factory, is something that looks like the granddaddy of all drills. Eighty times an hour a new cylinder block for a Ford engine slides up to the monster, and the monster bites into it. The cylinder block needs eighty-five holes chewed into it, each threaded like a screw on

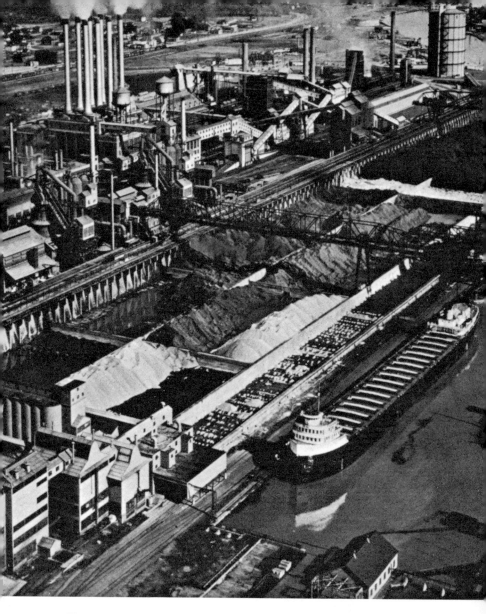

The Ford River Rouge plant can complete the whole process of converting ore into steel and steel into automobiles.

the inside. Granddaddy obliges. It takes him exactly seventeen seconds, while streams of cooling liquid pour over him and the cylinder block to keep them from getting too hot and sticking when the metal expands. Then the cylinder block moves on and Granddaddy sits back and waits for another one. A worker stands by to see that nothing goes wrong, but Granddaddy does the work. He does it just the same way each time and will go on doing it the same way till the cows come home.

Now Granddaddy and his companions cost thousands of dollars to begin with. But they save more thousands. Each can do the work of many skilled mechanics and do it more accurately than the most skilled. Each will pay for himself many, many times over as he turns out parts for cars to be sold to the general public.

Henry Ford found that it takes some of the most complicated and specialized machinery in the world to turn out cheap, simple cars with interchangeable parts. As he began to use this machinery, he was faced by a new mass-production problem. The machines could make parts *too* fast! Just moving the parts around the factory from one machine to another became a real headache.

Ford called in an expert in factory arrangement, Walter E. Flanders. "We want to make 10,000 cars this year," Ford told him in 1908. "But we're tripping over our own toes. Can you get us unsnarled from this traffic jam?"

"I can," said Flanders, "if you'll let me do things my way." And he went to work.

At once he broke up the old arrangement of machines, by which all the drills doing one job had been in one place, all the presses doing another off by themselves. He rearranged the machines into long lines. First came a machine to shape the first rough part, next the machine that did the next bit of work, and so on. Soon a rough bit of metal came in at one end, and a finished part came out at the other. The production line had been born. In three months Flanders had his lines working smoothly, and the 10,000 cars were finished two days ahead of schedule.

Still this was not good enough! Now the men in the assembly shop, where all the finished parts were put together, could not keep up with the production lines. Two other men who worked for Ford studied the problem through the next few years and came up with a brilliant idea. Why shouldn't the assemblers—the men who put the cars together—work in a long line the way the machines that made the parts did?

C. W. Avery and William Klann decided to try it. They took a bare frame, the skeleton of a car, and stood it in one end of the shop. Two hundred and fifty feet were cleared for their experiment. They hitched the frame by a long rope to a windlass that slowly wound the rope up and pulled the frame forward. As it moved along, six trained men began fastening on the parts that would make it a car. They walked beside it tightening bolts, or swarmed over it like squirrels to fit parts inside. When the skeleton reached the end of its 250-foot run, it had been turned into a finished car. More important, the time it took to complete the car had been cut in half.

Ford was delighted. He ordered two assembly lines set up at once. But soon an even newer improvement was added—an overhead conveyor belt, strong enough to lift the whole final assembly line off the factory floor and carry the auto frames along waist-high, where the men could add parts most easily. When these new assembly lines began to work in January, 1914, they cut the time of building a car from the twelve hours it had taken a year before to just over an hour and a half. And time saved meant money saved, because the same number of workmen could turn out many more cars. Prices could be made lower, to bring Fords within the reach of more people. The first Model T had sold for $850. The price went down steadily until, in 1917, it was only $360.

Model T Number 2,000,000 was built that year. Fords were spreading everywhere in the country, and every comedian on the vaudeville stage had a joke or two about "Lizzie." "The fellow who owns a second-hand Ford," the comedian might begin, "may not have a quarrelsome disposition. But he's always trying to start something." Or he might refer to a "noted magician, part of whose act is to make a horse vanish." Then he'd add, "But that's nothing! Look at Henry Ford!"

As for Ford songs, they ran on and on from 1914's cheerful statement that "The Little Ford Rambled Right Along," through 1915's warning that "You Can't Afford to Marry if You Can't Afford a Ford," up to 1928. That was when the Model T was finally replaced by the more up-to-date Model A, and singers chorused "Henry's Made a Lady out of Lizzie."

But before Lizzie turned into a lady, more than fifteen million Model T's had been built. With the folding top in place, the Model T stood seven feet high, but the wheelbase was so short it could turn on a circle of twelve-foot radius. Enthroned on the front seat, the driver saw no accelerator before him (the gas throttle was operated by hand on the steering wheel) and no gear shift. But this was not because he had a smooth automatic transmission, such as has taken the place of gears in most of today's cars. No, the pedals on the floor that weren't the brake were the controls of the "planetary transmission." Basically some of the new transmission systems use the same principles that the Model T system used. But the Model T "planetary transmission" was neither smooth nor automatic.

Very few drivers really understood just how this mysterious method of getting power from the engine to the wheels worked. But they didn't care, for work it did. "In its palmy days," writes Lee Strout White, who drove and loved an early Ford, "the Model T could take off faster than anything on the road. The reason was simple. To get under way, you simply hooked the third finger of the right hand around a lever on the steering column, pulled down hard, and shoved your left foot forcibly against the low-speed pedal; the car responded by lunging forward with a roar. After a few seconds of this turmoil you took your toe off the pedal, eased up a mite on the throttle, and the car, possessed of only two forward speeds, catapulted directly into high with a series of ugly jerks and was off on its glorious errand. The abruptness of this departure was never equaled in other cars of this period. The human leg was (and still is) incapable of letting in a clutch with anything like the abandon that used to send a Model T on its way. . . . Pushing down the Ford pedal was a simple, country motion . . . which came as natural as kicking an old door to make it budge."

The gas tank was under the front seat. When it had to be filled, the driver got out and so did anyone sitting with him, which made stopping for gas quite a chummy occasion. The first Model T's had no gas gauge. Every driver carried a stick, which he thrust through the hole in the tank to measure the height of his fuel. "The Ford driver," as Mr. White says, "flew blind. . . . He didn't know the temperature of his engine, the speed of his car, the amount of his fuel, or the pressure of his oil. . . . The dashboard of the early models was bare, save for an ignition key." A rear-view mirror could be bought as an extra, like a windshield wiper. "But most Model T owners weren't worried by what was coming from school of thought that used the reverse pedal to brake the car with—but you had to be careful, for the Ford could go from forward into reverse without a moment's hesitation, and you might find yourself wilting your fenders by backing into the car behind you.

As for cranking the Model T, this was something you had to learn by trial and error, hoping that you wouldn't acquire a Ford Fracture along the way. One problem was that Model T's always wanted to get started. If the emergency brake wasn't pulled all the way back, writes Mr. White, "the car advanced on you the instant the first explosion occurred and you would hold it back by leaning your weight against it. I can still feel my old Ford nuzzling me at the curb, as though looking for an apple in my pocket"—like the horse it had replaced.

These were the cars that became members of the family all over America. They were loved and laughed at, kicked and depended on.

Because of them back roads were paved, service stations became common, great new industries like oil and rubber appeared, and towns grew from crossroads to cities. For now, the farmer could come to town, and the city worker could live in the suburbs. Different parts of the country began to know each other. The tourists were coming, and many a family set off on its vacation determined to "See Pike's Peak or bust!"

TOURISTS, W
or employees
cars.

In 1903, h
H. Nelson J
Winton in S
wheels into th
Sixty-three da
The same yea
Fetch who ma
one-cylinder P
lunger" in tho
days. This was
for Tom Fetch
Packard Comp
other profession

But Nelson J
amateurs could
the professional

People might
or for the sake
easily and quickl

owner of an automobile would feel the urge to go touring, to explore what lay over the hills and far away. After he had covered the roads that could be driven in an afternoon, he'd try an all-day trip. Then would come the idea of a week's vacation spent in sightseeing. A century ago, traveling for pleasure was almost unheard of. The rich might perhaps make a tour of Europe, and ordinary folk might enjoy a once-in-a-lifetime honeymoon trip to Niagara Falls. When the automobile made it possible for everyone to travel for fun, people were as excited as if they'd been presented with a magic carpet.

In the early years of the century, when almost all country roads were potholes tied together by ruts, when gas stations and road markers didn't exist, travel-for-fun took quite a bit of getting ready. The best way was to do it in a group. While a lone motorist might be stranded by engine trouble or stuck help-

8 TOURISTS

THE HISTORY OF
as old as the hi
In 1900 Alexan
land to New Y
Chapin achieved
the little Olds
Auto Show from
these runs were

lessly in the mud, six or eight carloads could help each other out.

As more and more people bought automobiles, they formed themselves into auto clubs. The clubs tried to protect the motorist against the absurd laws that imposed five-mile-an-hour speed limits, for instance, or closed certain roads to motorists. In New York, Central Park was closed to cars until several gentlemen of the highest social standing drove in and got themselves arrested on purpose, to show how silly the rule was. They were officials of the New York Automobile Club. The clubs also worked hard for better roads. And whether they had planned to or not, they soon found themselves arranging tours for their members. One of the most important duties, in arranging a tour, was to provide a pilot—someone to ride in the first car who knew the way from one town to the next.

Local clubs arranged all-day runs for their

members. One from New York to Philadelphia was so successful that the daring New York club decided to put on a tremendous tour—tremendous, that is, for 1901. Motorists were to drive all the way from New York City to Buffalo, doing sixty-five miles each day. There they could enjoy a world's fair which Buffalo called the Pan-American Exposition and which President McKinley was planning to visit.

Alas, the weather was frightful. It rained and rained and rained, and of course there wasn't a closed car in the caravan. Day after day, soaked and discouraged motorists dropped out. The fifty-one mud-stained and battered vehicles that reached Rochester, New York, were greeted with dreadful news. President McKinley had been shot by a madman at the very Buffalo exposition they had been hastening to see. Sadly, the tourists turned toward home, and it was three more years before another big tour was organized.

This time things went much better. Local automobile clubs all over the country had now joined in one centralized organization, the American Automobile Association. If the AAA wanted to plan a big tour, each member club along the route of the tour would help out. Members of these local clubs did their best to see that city officials were impressed with the importance of the tour. They found places for tourists to sleep and provided guides to lead motorists over the roads in their territory. With this help along the way, the AAA announced a 1904 tour covering 1,318 miles, all the way from New York to St. Louis by way of Buffalo and Chicago. Why go to St. Louis? Well, another world's fair was being held there. Nothing seems to have attracted early tourists like a good world's fair!

This time, most of those who set out reached their destination. It took them seventeen days and a good many arguments. The tour to St.

This Buckmobile was one of the cars to start from New York in the St. Louis Tour of 1904.

Louis was not a race, American Automobile Association officials said firmly. It was a reliability run, to test the safety and sturdiness of the cars that were entered.

But some of the cars that were entered were driven by their manufacturers. There was a Mr. Pope in a Pope-Toledo, and a Colonel Pope in a Pope-Hartford, and Mr. Percy Pierce at the wheel of what was then called the Pierce Great Arrow. Each gentleman had entered the run as an amateur and had agreed not to race. Still, each felt a certain urge to see the car he had built and was driving cover the miles at a little better speed than his fellow amateurs.

Besides, at the very beginning of the tour the amateurs who had promised not to race had watched a most annoying incident. As the cars of the tour began to get under way, two men in a French Darracq had suddenly pulled around them and dashed up to the head of the line. Over the rear of the car fluttered a very impertinent sign: "St. Louis and back non-stop."

The roads were free, and the Darracq was free to drive on them, no matter how angry its boasts might make the members of the official tour. No one could stop the drivers of the French car. But the tourists comforted themselves with the thought that the Darracq never would drive to St. Louis and back non-stop. Actually, the Darracq did, according to the rules of a "nonstop" run in those days. Nonstop meant only that the engine of the car was not shut off. Drivers could stop, get out, eat, and even take naps.

Under these rules, the Darracq got to St. Louis in a week, ten days ahead of the tourists. It spent two days there with the motor running and made the return trip in six days. That may not be what we would call a nonstop run, but just the same a car engine that will run without stopping for days on end is something to be proud of, even today.

The American amateur drivers didn't try to keep up with the nonstop Darracq, but the thought of it chugging along their route ahead of them was another reason for them to try to show their best speed. Some of them began getting up earlier and earlier each morning, in order to be the first into the city where they were to spend the night.

Aside from the arguments over racing, the main problem of the tourists was the livestock with which they had to share the country roads.

When the driver of a 70-horsepower Peerless reached Buffalo, he found that he was being sued for frightening a valuable horse. In Toledo, Ohio, each member of the party was halted by a fierce-looking police officer, and handed a court summons for running over a dog. Only after each tourist had begun to declare that he was innocent did the "police officer" explain that this time it was all a joke, and that the "summons" was really an invitation to attend a party of the Toledo Automobile Club.

But of all the "critters" who wouldn't get off the road for a car, chickens were the worst. Every motorist had a certain number of "fowl murders" on his conscience, but one day saw the biggest bag of all. That was the time when the confetti car ran out of confetti. The confetti car was supposed to lead the way and mark the correct route for the tourists to follow. It carried a load of chopped-up paper that it sprinkled along the road, just the way the leader of a paper-chase does.

In Pontiac, Illinois, soon after leaving Chicago, the driver of the confetti car discovered that he had used up his supply, and no one had arranged for any more. But he was a resourceful man, and he decided that if cars could follow a trail of confetti, they could follow one made of kernels of corn. Off he went, therefore, scattering corn behind him. And out on the roads behind him came the chickens of all the farms he passed, delighted to find their favorite food suddenly appearing out of nowhere. Then came the tourists—and chicken after chicken became a traffic casualty. The last cars along the road followed feathers instead of confetti!

On another day, the confetti car had a plentiful supply of chopped-up paper, but an engine that was very far from powerful. Starting at the head of the line, it was passed by car after car. As the last of the tourists went by, they called out to the dogged driver, to ask why he didn't quit his job now that it was useless. "Perhaps someone will want to come back," said the confetti man hopefully, and went on with his chore. When the tourists compared notes that night, they discovered that every one of them had arrived at his destination by a different route.

Still it was a grand and glorious tour as the drivers who made the whole run agreed. And almost all did manage to complete the tour and reach St. Louis, although accidents happened up to the very last minute. There were even some accidents as cars crossed the bridge over the Mississippi coming into St. Louis. One car ran out of gas; another knocked a bicycle and its rider over; and a third ran into a coal truck. But no one was hurt, and St. Louis gave the tourists a wonderful welcome. Cars that had joined the tour along the way and local motorists shared a parade with the few who had made the whole trip. Astonished St. Louisans counted 300 vehicles altogether. After a week at the world's fair the tourists started home. Though some of the less daring took to the railroad, the more experienced—or enthusiastic—drivers set right out to drive all the way back.

One of the most experienced of all these enthusiasts was Charles J. Glidden. Mr. Glidden had been driving motorcars since motorcars first appeared. He had toured all over Europe and the United States, and had made his way across Canada by using railroad tracks when he ran out of roads. However, he did not bounce uncomfortably over the ties like the desperate drivers of the Thomas Flyer that crossed Siberia. Instead, he had special steel wheels made to fit the railroad tracks, and simply removed the rubber-tired wheels of his English Napier and changed them for steel railroad wheels.

Mr. Glidden was so impressed with the success of the 1904 tour to St. Louis that he offered to put up a huge trophy, like the Vanderbilt Cup. The American Automobile Association was to award it for a reliability run, not for a race. Each year a tour would be held to test how easily, comfortably and safely cars could cover the miles. Every driver must report the stops he made and the reasons—flat tire, broken drive chain, leaking gas line, or whatever it might be. There was to be no racing. Speed laws were to be obeyed, and no credit was to be allowed drivers for speed in reaching the end of each day's run. The Glidden trophy was to be awarded to the driver with the most nearly perfect score.

The first Glidden tour took place in July, 1905. Starting from New York, close to Central Park, the cars were to circle through New England to Bretton Woods, New Hampshire, and return—a total of 870 miles. But if Mr. Glidden had hoped that only amateur drivers would enter, he was doomed to disappointment. If the manufacturer of an automobile joined the American Automobile Association and paid his entrance fee for the tour, the AAA couldn't tell him not to. So when the cars entered for the tour gathered, Mr. Walter White was at the wheel of a White Steamer, and Mr. R. E. Olds was driving the Reo that he then built. Percy Pierce was once more present in a Pierce Great Arrow. Mr. Maxwell and Mr. Briscoe of the Maxwell-Briscoe Company were both there, and no less than three members of the Pope family turned up.

Perhaps Mr. Glidden hoped that the presence of ladies would keep the competition between the different manufacturers of cars from becoming too bitter. But this didn't work either. In fact, any influence the ladies might have had disappeared after Mrs. John Cuneo's accident. Mrs. Cuneo was bravely driving herself, but the tour had got no farther than Greenwich, Connecticut, about forty miles from New York, when she drove right through the rail of a bridge. Luckily the drop into the small stream below was not very great. Mrs. Cuneo and her car were fished out at once and were able to continue the run only slightly battered. But unfortunately a number of remarks about "women drivers" began to be heard. They were no funnier then than they are now, just a little newer. As a matter of fact, Mrs. Cuneo was a good enough driver to take part in a three-day racing meet in 1909 and to come in second with only Ralph De Palma ahead of her.

The first night of the 1905 Glidden tour was spent in Hartford, Connecticut, the home of the Popes, and Colonel Pope entertained at an elegant party. The next day's run to Boston was easy, and even the baggage trucks which carried the trunks arrived in time for the tourists to dress for dinner.

But as the motorists came into New Hampshire, they began to run into trouble. Neither
the people nor the horses of the Granite State
took kindly to automobiles, and a speed limit
of eight miles an hour was being enforced.
Near Dover, policemen disguised as workmen
were posted along the route of the tour, ready
with ropes to sling across the road and stop any
"speeder" tearing along at nine miles an hour.
Warned by friendly motorists in Conway, the
tourists crept cautiously through the trap. But
the slow speed caused some cars to stall, and
the whole procession was held up again and
again while the stalled cars were cranked. The
tourists did not enjoy New Hampshire's welcome.

Still, there were no really serious accidents
on the way to Bretton Woods, although there
were one or two incidents that made Mr. Glidden more certain than ever that racing must not

be allowed. Of course, the drivers involved declared that they hadn't been racing—they had
only been "comparing speed." Once, for instance, a Cadillac tried to pass a White Steamer.
The Steamer was kicking up quite a cloud of
dust, as every car did on a dry dirt road, and the
Cadillac driver could not see very far ahead.
Suddenly a narrow bridge appeared, almost
under his wheels. It was too late to stop. The
driver of the Cadillac tried to take the bridge
on two wheels. But since his vehicle was an
automobile and not a bicycle, it refused. Hap-
pily, he and his passengers were promptly
pulled out of the ditch, and the car was able
to continue.

More surprising, if not more dangerous, was
the experience of another motorist. Soon after
the party started back from Bretton Woods, a
sudden thunderstorm blew up. A group in a
Locomobile were caught with the top down,
and in 1905 it took more than the touch of a

finger to raise the top of a car. The family in the Locomobile didn't even try. They just drove on, looking for a farm or even a barn where they could take shelter before they were completely drenched. The driver pulled quickly into the first farmyard he saw, and drove as close to the house as he could get.

There on the porch was a man asleep in a rocking chair. The noise of the storm had not yet disturbed him, and the driver opened his mouth to shout and awaken him. Before the shout came out—a lightning bolt struck the house. It grounded with a flash and a bang right in front of the sleeper. More startled than Rip Van Winkle, the poor man jumped up, took one look at the car, and thought the devil-wagon was exploding before his eyes. He fled in terror into the house, and the driver of the Locomobile sat in the rain unable to explain what had happened. It must have been a long, long time before the idea of an automobile ride could be sold to *that* resident of New Hampshire!

Speed traps were not confined to New Hampshire, either, the tourists found out, for they ran into a particularly annoying one in a little town in Massachusetts. The local police were watching a stretch of road at the foot of a hill. If the tourists didn't speed over it, to get a good start, they couldn't get up the hill. If they did speed, they were promptly arrested. Six of them went to court and paid fines, one of them being poor Mrs. Cuneo.

But the motorists had their revenge. All of them decked their cars out with black crepe, as if for a funeral. They hired a band to lead them, and to the strains of a funeral march they drove at two miles an hour through the streets of that Massachusetts town. In front of the house of the constable who had arrested them they paused, and treated him to a quarter of an hour of this dismal serenade. When they went on their way finally, they felt so much better that they enjoyed one of the best day's motoring of all.

At the end of the tour, reports from the drivers were handed in. Then it was found that seven cars had made absolutely perfect scores. Which of the seven should receive Mr. Glidden's trophy? The AAA decided to let the members of the tour vote on the winner. Mr. Glidden's hopes of keeping the manufacturers of cars out of the tour suffered a blow, for Percy Pierce won by a wide margin.

The Pierce Great Arrow, driven by Percy Pierce, won the Glidden Tour in 1905.

Long Island Automotive Museum Photo

9   AMERICANS TAKE TO THE ROAD

THE NEXT FEW YEARS SAW THE GLIDDEN TOURS cover much of America. New England was visited again, and so were Canada and the Middle West. In other years the route lay through the South, or swung as far west as Denver, Colorado. The tourists enjoyed week ends at elegant summer resorts and suffered through mosquito-bitten nights of camping out. The 1906 tour was unlucky enough to have to share some of the roads it traveled with the United States Army which was holding practice maneuvers in New York's Adirondack Mountains. Heavy army equipment broke most of the small bridges along the way. Before Army engineers could rebuild them, the motorists had had to creep through detours over almost unused back roads. Even the official pilot cars broke down.

Hotel rooms were another problem. Sometimes there just weren't enough to go around. One night two gentlemen, faced with the uncomfortable prospect of sleeping in porch chairs, went over to the local jail and had themselves arrested as vagrants. The beds in the jail were not the most comfortable in the world, but they were better than porch chairs! On the 1909 tour to Denver, a special train of dining cars and sleepers took the same route. Every night the motorists drove to some wayside station and climbed aboard the train to sleep.

But the biggest trouble that the American Automobile Association had with the Glidden tours was over the rules. They were changed again and again, but indignant tourists always found something wrong with them. And no matter how they were changed, Percy Pierce went on winning. It was really rather discouraging for other contestants! In the end, automobiles had improved so much that many motorists turned in perfect scores, and it became very hard to pick the winner. One year there was a lawsuit over who deserved the prize.

Before the tours were discontinued in 1913, however, they had served their purpose well. Car buyers and car builders had been shown how important safety and sturdiness were. The need for better roads had been made clear. People had begun to talk about the idea of a road clear across the country, well kept up and marked all the way with signs—the Lincoln Highway. Most important of all, the fun and excitement of touring was interesting more and more people. Everyone wanted to take a tour, the longer the better.

And tour they did! Bellamy Partridge, author and motoring fan, has written the story of his tour across the continent in 1912. He and Mrs. Partridge and two friends set out from New York on July 13th, and reached San Diego, California, more than two months later. Their forty-horsepower six-cylinder Matheson had wallowed through mud and had been mired in puddles the size of small ponds. In the East, where many places were building better roads for the sake of future tourists, these particular tourists had had to follow unmarked detours, steering by the line of telegraph poles from one town to another. In the West, they had learned to watch out for prairie-dog holes, which could undermine the rutted tracks that were called roads. Then a wheel would go down in a hole with an awful jar and break a spring.

The men had repaired the jammed steering gear themselves, and at another time had helped a busy blacksmith finish shoeing a team of mules so he could work on the car. Tire trouble had bothered them almost every day. A flat tire still meant pulling the tire off the metal rim, taking the tube out, and patching it with a square of rubber that you cemented to the tube by heating it with a vulcanizing kit. They learned to carry a block and tackle with which to be pulled out of ditches, extra gasoline, and several days' supply of food and water. They spent the night on farms or ranches, or out under the stars.

Of course, they got thoroughly lost from time to time. One night, in a little town that went to bed with the sun, they had to hunt up the railroad station and read the signs there to tell east from west. Another time they got directions from a forest ranger and rode off triumphantly, only to find several hours later that they had driven in a circle. For when they stopped for directions again, the same ranger came out to help them!

But they had a wonderful time, these pioneers like the Partridges. They were seeing America, from the peaceful little villages of New England to the wide prairies and the great ranges of the Rockies. Little by little, as their numbers grew, things began to change. In 1916 the Federal Government agreed to help the states pay for highways. Now the cost of keeping up roads would not have to be paid by the farmers who lived along the way. Since all of America was beginning to use the American roads, the government of all America would help in building and repairing them.

Not that the roads improved very fast! In 1921 a young lady from Boston, Miss Winifred

Dixon, published a book about her tour through the Southwest. She and another daring young lady had traveled alone. This adventurous pair found the going as hard as the Partridges had in 1912. Their big Cadillac stuck in mud holes and had to be hauled out by mule teams. Once it stalled in the middle of a rising river they had been trying to ford, for bridges were still few and far between. The girls leaped out and made the shore safely, leaving the car behind, with all their possessions swirling about in it. It wasn't till a day later that a mechanic with a block and tackle could haul it out. The repairs took a week.

But the girls went on. In Texas they met herds of sheep wandering along the roads. At the sight of a car, these silly creatures dashed back and forth with frenzied "Baa-aa-aas." Finally the automobile stopped and the sheep were led slowly by. In cattle country, ranch fences ran right across the roads, for the ranchers found this much easier and cheaper than running their fences along the roads. Where the road went through, there was a gate. This gate had to be opened for each car and carefully closed again, so that one man's cattle did not invade the pastures of another ranch. Sometimes there were several gates in a single mile!

Where ranch land turned to mountains, narrow roads climbed along canyons with no wall on the outside, and a drop of hundreds of feet waiting for a careless driver. There were special rules of etiquette on these roads. When two cars met, the one that was climbing had the right of way. The other had to back cautiously uphill until it reached a place wide enough for the two to pass.

Our young ladies from the East developed wrists of steel as they wrenched at the steering wheel to guide their big car around tight curves, or jounced over rough tracks trying to

follow the ruts that looked the safest. Except
in a few big cities, there were no hotels. Sometimes the tourists were able to find a night's
lodging with a kindly family, but often they
pitched the little tent they carried with them,
and camped out. Though they heard rumors of
bandits, they met no one more unkind than
the traffic judge who fined them for speeding
on one of the few bits of good road they came
across. Polite cowboys went out of their way
to offer help when the gumbo roads mired the
car.

Right through the years that treacherous
gumbo mud was the motorist's nightmare until
paved roads finally put an end to it. It was the
same mud that the New York-to-Paris racers
washed off their car with a fire hose. In 1912,
the Partridges had met it first when a sudden
rainstorm came up as they drove a gumbo road
in the Middle West. Before they knew what
was happening, their automobile had skidded

clear around and was pointing back the way
they had come. Mr. Partridge climbed out to
put the tire chains on and landed flat on his
back. He finally got the chains on by staying
on his hands and knees, for the mud was so
slippery he fell down every time he tried to
stand up. In 1919 Sinclair Lewis, the famous
author, described it as "mud mixed with tar,
flypaper, fish, glue and well-chewed chocolate-
caramels." Miss Dixon and her friend found
that if it dried on the car, it had to be chipped
off with a chisel.

But in spite of all the difficulties, what fun
the early tourists had! A long tour was a real
adventure. As the girls from Boston drove
through the Southwest they learned to expect
one greeting. Sooner or later, everyone they
met would say admiringly and a little envi-
ously, "Well! You're a long way from home!"

"Indeed we are!" the girls always replied,
and their new friends would smile back at them

as if they, too, were sharing the fun of traveling and exploring the world.

Today, we sometimes spin along our super-highways and hardly notice when we pass from one state to another. But in the early years, everyone shared the thrill of pioneering. Never before had so many people enjoyed travel and the wonders waiting everywhere to be discovered—the Indian villages of the Southwest, the great wheat farms of the prairie states, the sleepy old towns of the South, or the beautiful National Parks, like Yellowstone and Yosemite which were not opened to motorists until 1915. As Americans took to the roads, America was beginning to learn about itself.

And because Americans were taking to the roads, America began to change. Today, every city has a fringe of pleasant suburbs around it. Families can bring up their children outside the crowded cities, where there are trees and lawns, while fathers commute to their work in the busy center. In one small town in Connecticut, for instance, there now live many people whose offices are in New York, more than sixty miles away. But an old gentleman has told me that in the 1890s it took all day to travel to the county seat just ten miles away. That meant hitching the big farm horses to the wagon early in the morning and returning in the late afternoon. The family made the journey only three or four times a year.

In that town, children learned their lessons in a little one-room schoolhouse. The teacher had pupils ranging in age from six to sixteen. One teacher taught everything from reading to algebra. Ten of these one-room schoolhouses were dotted around the township. Most of the children walked several miles to school, rain or shine, snow or fine weather, carrying their books and their lunches. Part of the teacher's job was to keep the wood stove going through the cold winter days.

Today a fine modern school stands in the center of the township. Its big gymnasium is used by the children for play games in the daytime and in the evening it is used by the grownups for all kinds of meetings and activities. Well-trained teachers are in charge of the separate grades and special instructors in art and music and shopwork come in several days each week. They drive their cars to other schools on other days. All this has happened because every morning big yellow busses cruise for miles through the township picking up the children near their houses and bringing them to school. Every day several mothers drive to school and help serve the children a hot lunch. Big trucks deliver the food, and others bring the oil for the furnace that heats the building. It all seems so easy that no one ever stops to think how the automobile is helping children get the education they will need when they are grown up.

When the family car goes to market, it shows

us another change in American life that we owe to the automobile. Sixty years ago farm families grew almost all the things they ate. At harvest time women worked for weeks on end to can and preserve food that would carry them through the winter. It was hard work, too, as anyone who has tried to keep up with a garden patch knows. Even in the cities, fresh fruits and vegetables were rare in the winter and so high-priced that only the rich could afford them. I remember my mother telling me that one of the Christmas treats was an orange in each child's stocking.

But now big trucks pound north all winter long, bringing fresh foods to market. The terrible diseases that came from not getting enough of the right foods have almost disappeared. Our whole nation is growing up healthier and stronger because good food can now be bought cheaply everywhere all year round.

Perhaps the biggest change that the automobile has made, though, is in bringing people together. It is hard for us to realize today how lonely life was for many people only sixty years ago. When we try to imagine life two or three generations back, we are apt to think of the merry times people had at square dances and husking bees and church socials, or the neighborly atmosphere of the general store where men gathered around the stove to sit and chat through a winter day.

But those happy gatherings were remembered so well because they happened so seldom. In between them, farm families lived very much to themselves—and up to 1920, over half the population of the United States lived on farms. People met at church on Sunday and sometimes at market, but they did not meet often at any other time. Visiting wasn't easy—the horses were needed for farm work, and a neighbor who lived four miles away was more distant than a friend twenty miles away today. Country living in the old days certainly had many joys, but it had hardships, too. One that we would find hardest would be the difficulty of seeing old friends, or making new ones.

Today with television and radio in many homes and with newspapers delivered by truck, even the smallest village in the country is able to know what is happening the world over. Sixty years ago many people lived in ignorance of events that might change their lives. They had to live so, for there was just no way of getting information to them. In the 1890s a writer, Mr. Marion Hughes, lived in a little town in Arkansas named Hatton Gap. The citizens of Hatton Gap voted in the election of 1896, when William Jennings Bryan ran for President against William McKinley. But they saw so little news of these two candidates, reports Mr. Hughes, that their votes were as follows; Bryan, 15; Andrew Jackson, 12; Jeff Davis, 9; George Washington, 8; Moses, 6;

John the Baptist, 3; Daniel Boone, 2; William McKinley, 1.

No town in America can live that far out of the world today! The automobile and the good roads that it has brought have tied all the sections of our nation closer together. East and west, north and south, city and country, people understand each other better, for they have visited back and forth and learned to know each other.

10 PAST, PRESENT AND WHAT NEXT?

THE HISTORY OF THE AUTOMOBILE IS A HISTORY
of constant change. No one can tell exactly
what is coming next, just as no one has ever
been absolutely sure who should get credit for
originating the idea of the motorcar. Shall we
start on the evening of September 21, 1893,
when Frank Duryea cranked the first American-
made gasoline car? It ran twenty-five feet down
Spruce Street in Springfield, Massachusetts, and
then stalled. After another cranking, it covered

two hundred feet, and then Mr. Duryea decided that he and his "motor carriage" had done enough for one day.

That was one "first time," but it wasn't *the* "first time." Before it, had come the day in 1885 when Karl Benz drove his tricycle about the streets of Mannheim, Germany, using his own design of four-cycle engine. And Benz had been preceded by George Selden and his patent application for a vehicle with a Brayton-cycle motor on May 8, 1879. And before Selden came another American, George Brayton, who actually ran an engine powered by gasoline in 1874, though the gas was not exploded but burned slowly. And before Brayton was an Austrian, Siegfried Marcus, who ran a hand cart with a two-cycle gasoline engine on April 9, 1865, the very day that General Lee surrendered at Appomattox Courthouse. And before Marcus came a Frenchman, Jean Joseph Etienne Lenoir, who fitted a tank of illuminating gas into a wagon, pumped the gas to an engine, and ran this vehicle in the suburbs of Paris about 1862.

Nor can we stop there, if we take steam into account. In England, Richard Trevithick had a passenger-carrying steam-vehicle running in 1801, which gave rise to a number of steambusses. And in 1769 a Frenchman, Nicolas Joseph Cugnot, produced a three-wheeled steam wagon. It impressed the French Government so much that they ordered one from Cugnot, designed to pull a cannon. It could do three miles an hour. But it would have been beaten, on a breezy day, by the two-masted square-sailed wind carriage which the Dutch saw run at The Hague in 1600, making twenty miles an hour.

So you might say that our story has no beginning, and certainly it has no end. But it has a fine, exciting middle. For the automobile has not just changed itself as the years have gone by. It has changed the way we live. In 1893, when the first Duryea put-putted 225 feet, even in 1895 when an improved Duryea won the Chicago race, America was a very different place from what it is today. Says Philip Van Doren Stern in his *Pictorial History of the Automobile,* "The only inventions (in 1893) that affected the average person's everyday life were the steam engine, the telegraph, the printing press, the camera, the sewing machine, and the bicycle, all of which had been in use before the Civil War. Newer inventions, like the telephone, the electric light, the phonograph, and the Linotype, were not yet far enough along in their development to be in general use. If one wanted to take a long journey in 1893, he could travel only by rail or ship. Then, when he arrived at his destination, he had to use a slowly moving horse-drawn vehicle of some kind to get beyond walking distance of his point of arrival. He had to travel on schedule, and he could go only where some means of public transportation was readily available."

And today? In 1949 Lloyd Morris wrote, in his book *Not So Long Ago,* about the changes the automobile had made by the middle of the Twentieth Century: "Less than sixty years after the first native horseless carriage rattled over a Massachusetts road, one million Americans were employed in the manufacture of motor vehicles and parts. Eight million more were employed in related automotive fields." (This would take in the gas station operators, the workers in the oil industry and the tire companies, and so on.) "Approximately one of every six business firms in the United States was in some way dependent, for its profits, on the automotive industry." And since 1949, the automobile industry has grown, not shrunk.

Now each year millions and millions of cars come off the great assembly lines of the automobile companies. In Ford's 1200-acre River Rouge factory, Ford ore ships deliver iron ore from the Mesabi range at one end, and finished cars drive out at the other. Inside the plant is a glass factory that can make enough glass a year to stretch a sheet, four-foot wide, from New York to New Orleans. It doesn't make enough for the Ford Company, though, which buys as much glass again from other suppliers. Just to keep the Rouge plant clean wears out seven thousand mops a month, and its telephone system handles seven and a half million calls a year. The final assembly line, stretching around eight hundred feet, is timed to turn a bare frame into a finished car in eighty-seven minutes. And in addition to what the Ford Company makes itself, it buys parts and such things as paint, upholstery materials and insulation from six thousand other independent manufacturers scattered all over the country.

Beside America's sixty million passenger cars, roll its millions of trucks. Into Washington Market in New York come 1,600 a night, bringing food for the city. Out of Des Moines, Iowa, one newspaper sends 300 trucks to deliver its morning paper to readers all over the state. In Sacramento, California, one furniture store owns seventy trucks. They cover enough miles each month to go three times around the world. Refrigerator trucks carrying meat, tank trucks carrying milk, tank trucks carrying oil, frozen-food trucks carrying fish from New England or strawberries from Florida, moving vans, trailer trucks that measure fifty feet from bumper to bumper and carry twenty tons of freight—all crisscross our nation.

Again, it's impossible to say just when the trucking business began. Some of the first electrics that Hiram Maxim designed for Colonel Pope were delivery trucks to carry goods from the stores of Hartford, Connecticut, to its homes. But an old friend of ours had a great deal to do with showing how trucks could be used for long runs. This was none other than Roy Chapin, who drove the Oldsmobile runabout from Detroit to New York in 1901.

During World War I, President Wilson made Chapin head of the Highway Transport Commission. Chapin knew that our government had ordered thirty thousand trucks for delivery to France, where they were needed to bring ammunition, food and clothing to our soldiers. Ordinarily these trucks would have been put on railroad flatcars for shipment to the Atlantic ports. But Chapin had another idea. He ordered the trucks loaded with war supplies and driven to the seacoast. It was one of the first feats of long-distance hauling.

For war and the automobile have influenced each other, too. Where previous wars had seen generals mounted on chargers, World War I found them driving about in staff cars. General

Sheridan made his famous dash from Winchester to the battlefront on a jet black Morgan gelding with three white feet. But General Pershing's military journeys were made either in a Locomobile limousine, or a Dodge named Daisy. The self-propelled tanks of World War I gave birth to the massive armored divisions of World War II. Cavalry regiments found themselves "motorized," and even the army mule had to make way for the jeep.

After the attack on Pearl Harbor in December, 1941, the American automobile industry went to war along with our troops. Early in 1942 production of cars for civilians stopped completely. Instead, the plants turned out tanks, planes, engines, and army trucks, like the ones that tore across the Red Ball Highway in France bringing supplies to Eisenhower, Patton, Bradley, and our English allies for the final thrust against Hitler's armies. At home, gasoline was rationed, tires were rationed, and every motorist was taught to ask himself, as he climbed into his car, "Is this trip necessary?"

Many, many trips *were* necessary, for the automobile had made itself so important a part of American life that the country could not run without it. Trains, subways, streetcars and public busses could not begin to carry to their work the men and women who made the products America had to have to win the war. Car pools were formed, so that groups of people rode to work together instead of each in his own car. But even before the war was over, as early as 1944, the War Production Board had to permit the building of light trucks for civilian use, just to keep goods coming to market.

The war influenced the passenger-car industry in another way. It took quite a long time, after it was over, for American companies to get their enormous plants ready to make passenger

automobiles again. In 1946 only about two million cars were built. Perhaps that sounds like
a lot, but it didn't begin to fill the orders from
people who had nursed pre-war cars along for
years and wanted new ones. The automobile
industry has since built more than six million
cars in each of several years and almost eight
million in 1955. Indeed, if you count trucks
and busses, you will find that more than nine
million vehicles were turned out that year.

So foreign cars began to come in. City dwel-
lers found that midget cars like the English
Austin, the French Renault and the German
Volkswagen were handy in the teeming traffic
of urban streets. And then there were the sports
cars—English Jaguars and MGs, Italian Alfa-
Romeos and Ferraris, German Mercedes-Benzes
and many others.

These gleaming, speedy machines brought
back to motoring some of the thrill of the early
days. The useful, necessary automobile that gets

you where you want to go and can be quickly patched up at any service station is still the car that most people need and buy. But sports-car fans have begun to find out that driving can be more than just covering miles. It can be fun.

In the first years of the century, every driver knew his car and its engine intimately. Quite often he'd had it apart and put it together himself, like the doctors who taught themselves the anatomy of the automobile by "thorough dissection." Of course it was messy work, but it gave car owners an understanding of how their vehicles worked and what could be expected of them, plus a fine confidence in their own skill. When Miss Dixon and her friend were touring the West at the beginning of the 1920s, their proudest hour occurred when they took apart the ignition system of their Cadillac, fixed it, and got it back together again with the help of a nail file and a Chippewa Indian they happened to meet.

So today, the real sports-car fan knows and loves his automobile. It may be a hot rod he has tenderly "souped up" himself. It may be a fire-engine-red MG whose motor has known hours of careful polishing with a cork dipped in brass polish and abrasive. It may be a great old sports car carefully reclaimed and rebuilt by a loving owner, like Ken Purdy's 1912 Mercer runabout. One of Mr. Purdy's joys is to take the Mercer out on the road and trundle along at a comfortable forty miles an hour until a curious carload pulls up beside him to stare and exclaim. Mr. Purdy allows them to goggle for a few minutes and then—bang into third gear goes the Mercer from its cruising fourth speed and shows its heels to the astonished public just as it did when it was owned by Barney Oldfield!

Sports cars are beginning to have an influence on the mass-produced American automobile.

Every owner of an unusual car knows that his conveyance fascinates the general public. The question, "Hey! What kind of a car is that?" is as familiar to him as "Git a horse!" was to his grandfather. Usually the owner is happy to discuss his beloved speedster, for his pride in it is matched by his technical knowledge of engine design and performance. To a sympathetic listener he can talk for hours of carburetors and camshafts, engine capacity and compression-ratio, springs and super-chargers. A good sports-car driver often drives by ear, listening to the tune his engine plays for any discordant notes that can mean trouble ahead. This new interest in driving-for-fun has already started Ford and Chevrolet to turning out Thunderbirds and Corvettes to appeal to the sports-car market. The experimental models used by American companies to test new ideas have been getting a "sports-car look."

Road racing is coming back, too. In Watkins Glen, New York, in California and in Florida thousands of folk have turned out to see the speedy sports cars streak by just as they did when Louis Wagner, Joe Tracy, and George Robertson contended for the Vanderbilt Cup. European sports cars are still the leaders, but Briggs Cunningham of Connecticut has challenged the Europeans with a hand-built American car using a stepped-up Chrysler engine. Cunninghams have competed with honor in the great French race at Le Mans.

What the future will bring, no one knows. But as our new turnpikes and superhighways are built, not only speed but safety and ease of handling will become more and more important. There are those who believe that the day of the piston engine will soon pass. In 1950 an English Rover with a gas-turbine engine took the road. Clutchless, gearless, without pistons, cylinders or crankshaft, it tore down an airport runway at nearly one hundred miles an hour, its turbine spinning at forty thousand revolutions per minute. Two years later a gas-turbine Rover did better than a hundred and forty miles an hour. At present the problem is that the gas turbine uses up its fuel too fast. But engineers are hard at work on this. General Motors has built two Firebirds, using gas turbines for power, and in 1956 the second was shown to the public in the Motorama. By re-capturing heat from the exhaust to warm the incoming air, the engine is made more efficient.

Still, the atomic engine may beat it yet. In 1953 Ford announced that its laboratories were working on the development of an atomic car. Perhaps with atom power, steam will come back. For, as the atomic submarine *Nautilus* has shown, the easiest way to use atomic energy for transport is by converting it to steam power.

In the meantime, America's millions of cars, trucks and busses stream along its highways and byways like the blood in our veins and arteries. The plaything of the rich has become the necessary means of transportation for Americans everywhere. Less than fifty years after Mrs. Belmont's automobile party in Newport, the hundred millionth American automobile was built. Some Americans, indeed, have done even more than use their cars to get from their homes to wherever they want to go. They have hitched their homes to their cars--as trailers--and have taken them right along with them.

Americans traveling abroad have refused to give up their favorite means of getting around, and every year the number of cars rented by tourists in Europe takes an upward jump. European builders are using American mass production methods more and more widely. England is now making more than twice as many cars as before World War II.

So the men with the dream, the "crackpots" and tinkerers, have seen their ideas change the world. The world did not welcome the change in the beginning, for people are apt to cling to old ways and old habits. The automobile seemed just a fad, at first. "If it should displace the horse," thundered Colonel Henry Watterson of Kentucky in 1900, "it can only be for a time."

But there were those who saw the future more clearly than Colonel Watterson. There was Hiram Maxim on his bicycle, dreaming of a nation bound together by the vehicle that could take any man where he wanted to go. There was Ransom Olds, shocking the solid businessmen of New Jersey by declaring that the horse and buggy were doomed. There was Henry Ford working nights on his buggy-seated bicycle-wheeled oddity, giving up his job to keep on experimenting. And there was Frank Duryea who calmly told a reporter after he had tested his improved "buggyaut" in 1894, "Nothing remains now but to perfect the details."

People have been perfecting them for more than sixty years, for not even the brightest dream becomes reality without long years of hard work. As early as 1900 an enthusiastic manufacturer advertised that he built "the perfect automobile"—but his company has long since vanished from the scene.

No one has built the perfect automobile, and every auto-maker today believes that something new and better always lies ahead. The quaint horseless carriage has gone to join the buggy it replaced, and when nuclear-powered, radar-controlled monsters speed over the superhighways of tomorrow, today's sleek cars will seem as odd as any of the old ones.

But the story is all one, the story of time and distance conquered and people brought together. No matter how strange and wonderful the cars of the future may be, they will owe their existence to the "crackpots" and tinkerers, the men who dreamed and the men who worked, the demon drivers and the painstaking engineers, whose story this is.